NATIVE AMERIC

CW00501285

NAVAJO CULTURE

AND THE

UNBREAKABLE CODE

By

Carol Dean

About the Author

My name is Carol Dean and I'm married with two adult children, and five grandchildren and we all live in the North East.

I started to write children's stories to entertain my children when they were young on rainy weekends or school holidays. My son writing stories about ghosts or vampires, and my daughter drawing pretty pictures. Nothing to do with the story but very pretty.

And this is where my Granny Ridley and Charlie Dryden stories first appeared.

Charlie Dryden's crime/adventure stories have since developed into an exciting series of books for 9-15 year olds. My funny Granny Ridley series for 7-10 year olds now has a further nine books. Plus PC Polly, my commissioned work, has since made an amusing addition for 7-10 year olds to have a good giggle over.

Many other characters have appeared and entertained various age groups, (adults included) in the shape of dinosaurs, spiders, teddy bears, a panda, unicorns, a few aliens and a friendly ghost there too. My Native American series of books are proving popular with adults and young teens too and I am delighted to say that all my books are selling in many countries around the world. Literally worldwide which is brilliant.

All of which you can find out more about on my website www.caroldeanbooks.com or follow me on Facebook.

ISBN 979-8-87894-810-4

Cover Images

Sarah A. Doidge artist QS:P170,Q56524451

USMC Archives from Quantico, USA

Liz West from Boxborough, MA

Also By Carol Dean

NATIVE AMERICAN SERIES

Comanche Life
A Man Called Sitting Bull
Geronimo and Cochise – Two Apache Legends
The Trail of Tears
Quanah Parker One Man Two Worlds
They Too Played Their Part
Where Everyone Knows Her Name
The Footsteps They Left Behind
Navajo Culture and the Unbreakable Code

THE WILD WEST

Days of the Old Wild West

CHARLIE DRYDEN SERIES

Charlie Dryden's Cricket Ball
Help Me Charlie Dryden
Charlie Dryden Finds a Bone
Charlie Dryden and the Charnwood Abbey Ghost
Charlie Dryden and the Guardian
Beware Charlie Dryden
Charlie Dryden and the Stolen Roman Standard

DINOSAUR STORIES

Dinosaur Stories
Reggie Learns a Lesson
Herbie's Big Day

Terry Comes Out of His Shell
Spike Gets a New Sister
Deano and the Baby Dinosaur

STORIES FOR EVERYBODY

Sophie the Suffragette
Webster Swings into Action
The Day the Ghost Got Scared
Amelia Flurry and the Legend of the Unicorn
Mr Mortimer Meets the Aliens

PC POLLY

PC Polly the Police Lady
Be Safe Be Seen PC Polly

PC Polly on Patrol
PC Polly and the Mini Police

CHRISTMAS STORIES

Santa Steams Ahead
Santa and the Magic Dust
The Day Santa Met Santa

GRANNY RIDLEY SERIES

Granny Ridley Tries Exercise
Granny Ridley Knows the Way
Granny Ridley Goes on a Trip
Granny Ridley in the Snow
Granny Ridley and the Alien

Granny Ridley Helps Out
Granny Ridley Tries Knitting
Granny Ridley Has a Weekend Away
Granny Ridley and Wolfie
Granny Ridley Gets the Runs

YOUNG READERS

Peter the Panda is Hungry

Teddy Has Lost His Growl

WAR STORIES

Ponsonby-Smallpiece - The Legend

You can find all Carol's books on her website www.caroldeanbooks.com.

CONTENTS

FOREWORD

It's not all that long since returning from a holiday of a lifetime which we called our *'American Adventure 2023'*. And it was during this holiday that I came to the decision to pay tribute to the Navajo Nation for their tremendous efforts during WWII.

I am delighted to say that part of the *'American Adventure 2023'* was spent in Monument Valley, the Navajo land. What better place to spend some time steeped in history and see those red rock monuments gloriously nestled under a perfectly blue cloudless sky.

John Wayne was absent from the scenery, naturally. But standing there trying to take it all in is impossible. It's just too vast and too beautiful to take in never mind record it on photographs.

But you can still stand there and imagine Mr Wayne riding across this beautiful landscape. Which he did in many of John Ford's films.

The Navajo have names for each of the rock formations and it's true, you could actually see the elephant or the waving hands looming above you, and making your eyes water with the majesty of it all.

But these lands have been the home to the Navajo Nation for generations and are considered sacred to them, as they believe that the lands have an energy that helps heal them.

The Tribal Park was a milestone in Indigenous history. 27,425 square mile (71,000 square kilometres) of territory in the Four Corners region of the United States.

And the Four Sacred Mountains of the Navajo are made up with the four mountains along the boundaries of the Navajo Nation stretching across modern day Colorado, New Mexico and Arizona.

The Four Sacred Mountains of the Diné Nation

According to Navajo belief, each mountain is assigned a colour and direction and is seen as a deity that provides essential resources for Navajo livelihood.

- Blanca Peak (*Sisnaajiní* — **White** Shell Mountain) in Colorado associated with the East

- Mount Taylor (*Tsoodził* — **Blue** Bead or Turquoise Mountain) in New Mexico associated with the South

- San Francisco Peaks (*Dook'o'oosłííd* — **Yellow** - Abalone Shell Mountain) in Arizona associated with the West

- Hesperus Mountain (*Dibé Nitsaa* — **Black** - Big Mountain Sheep) in Colorado associated with the North
  Wikipedia

The rock formations can be seen for miles standing between 400 and 1,200 feet tall forming part of the Colorado plateau.

What was once a basin became a plateau. Natural forces of wind and water eroded the land over the last 50 million years cutting into, and peeling away, at the surface of the plateau. This erosion wore down the differing layers of soft and hard rock and slowly revealed the natural wonders of Monument Valley as we see it today. Through the valley you can see buttes (meaning an isolated hill with steep sides) rising sometimes 1,000 feet from the ground. These buttes are also known as monuments giving the valley its name and making it a popular tourist attraction.

Monument Valley was the first of its kind thanks to the forward thinking of the Navajo Nation Tribal Council. The valley was established in 1958 and it was the first Tribal Park of its kind and has since paved the way for other tribes to create protected zones.

The site is not a national park, like nearby Canyonlands in Utah, and the Grand Canyon in Arizona, but one of six Navajo-owned tribal parks. What's more, the valley floor is still inhabited by Navajo — 30 to 100 people, depending on the season, who live in houses without running water or electricity.

© Carol Dean – Holiday photograph

Technical stuff over, Monument Valley has to be seen to be believed. We have always wanted to visit and this year, 2023, we got our wish. We met Navajo's. They escorted us through the valley explaining the names and the geology of the valley itself.

It's obvious that they love this land. It's huge, hot, dusty, desolate and you cannot travel unescorted across it. Mainly because that's just an insult to the Navajo should you try to. But also extremely stupid, as without help and knowledge, it's a land that could kill you. Very quickly.

But there is so much more to the Navajo than just Monument Valley as you will see through the pages of this book. The phrase 'they helped win the war' has the makings of the truth to it.

See what you think.

Carol Dean

Friendship

NAVAJO LIVES

I can't really start this tribute to the Navajo Nation without mentioning their generations of history on this land of theirs. We often forget that Native Americans from all tribes have been around for a very long time in what we now know as United States of America. So it seems fitting to start this tribute right at the beginning of it all.

The word 'Navajo' (pronounced na·vuh·how) is partially Spanish and comes from the Tewa Pueblo word navahu'u meaning *'farm fields in the valley'*. They were also referred to as Apaches de Nabajo which means *'Apaches who farm in the valley'*. This was shortened to Navajo.

The Navajo (Diné – The People) are part of the Athabascan speaking peoples believed to have originated in Asia and who crossed into North America via the frozen Bering Strait during the previous Ice Age, about 38,000 years ago. Over thousands of years, the Athabascans traveled southward beginning in about 1000 A.D. When the Bering Strait melted, the sea level rose, and they were trapped.

There were four original clans of the Navajo people

- Kinyaa'áanii (*The Towering House clan*)
- Honágháahnii (*One-walks-around clan*)
- Tódich'ii'nii (*Bitter Water clan*)
- Hashtł'ishnii (*Mud clan*)

    Wikipedia

Public Domain Image

Public Domain Image

The Navajo led a fairly peaceful relationship and co-existence with other tribes. Like most Native Americans, they did trade and they did raid among the other tribes in their area, such as the Apache, Comanche, and Hopi. The Navajo relationship with the Spanish in those days, could be described as *'tense but largely peaceful'*.

But Navajo culture is different to others. Leadership is arranged through clans which are 'matrilineal kinship' groups. *'A person's lineage is his or her line of ancestors. So matrilineal means basically "through the mother's line", just as patrilineal means "through the father's line" '*. Wikipedia

Children are considered born into the mother's family and gain their status from her and her clan alone. And any older brother, again through their tradition, has an influence on the upbringing of the child or children.

And in order to be considered to become a member of the Navajo Nation you must be at least one quarter Navajo to be enrolled.

Traditionally, the Navajo were farmers of vegetables, including beans, squash, and corn, which grew in many colors and was eaten dried (and ground) or fresh. These vegetables continue to be of huge importance to their health and lifestyle today.

Indian Corn
Steve Snodgrass from Shreveport, USA https://commons.wikimedia.org/wiki/File:Indian_Corn.jpg
https://creativecommons.org/licenses/by/2.0/legalcode

Public Domain Image

Women would gather varieties of nuts each year, plus foods from the land e.g. pumpkins, wild onions and prickly pear would add to their diet.

But what they really love is fry-bread. This particular food item stems from the Long Walk, which you will read about later in the book, when the government gave them flour, salt, water, lard, sugar, powdered milk and baking powder for cooking. Fry-bread was created out of those ingredients and has been a popular staple food since symbolizing, perseverance and strength. Having tried it at Monument Valley during a visit to a Navajo Cook-Out, I can see why. It was delicious. Very filling too.

3

Frybread
Anonymous https://commons.wikimedia.org/wiki/File:Frybread.jpg
https://creativecommons.org/licenses/by-sa/3.0/legalcode

The Navajo hunted deer and other small mammals for protein. Today sheep are raised in the territory for wool needed for weaving, and mutton is one of the tribe's most popular food sources.

Public Domain Image

However, the eating of fish and most water birds and animals is forbidden, and raw meat is taboo. Navajos will never cut a melon with the point of a knife. They never comb their hair at night. And no matter how crowded a hogan (Navajo dwelling) may be with sleeping figures, no Navajo may step over someone sleeping.

Navajo Hogans

Hogans were their homes and they provided a safe place to escape from the extremes in their environment. Hogans were common until the late 20th century, when timber homes replaced the traditional style, but these structures can still be seen today.

A hogan is a traditional one roomed dwelling. Logs were cut into lengths which would form eight sides of the building. There are no windows.

The straight sides of logs would be about shoulder height, with the logs will get shorter and shorter so that they make a kind of rounded roof.

Each log had to be notched so that they would fit together snugly and tightly. In the centre of the roof there would be a hole left open for smoke. Other than the door, this would be the only opening.

Dirt was crammed into any gaps between the logs to keep the cold out in winter and the heat in, in summer, with more dirt added to the roof for further insulation.

The doorway always faced east with wooden hunting bows hung inside and out for protection and the last item might be a blanket as a door cover.

Navajos always have had very strong family bonds. Even if a family member moved away from the reservation. It made no difference. The family ties are there and will not be broken.

Circumstances sometimes meant that a family member had to find work away from the reservation. But they would always send money home to help those who are still living on the reservation.

At the 2000 census, there were 864 people, 207 households, and 174 families living in Monument Valley without electricity or water. In 2020, the number of tribal members increased to 399,494 – making the Navajo Nation the largest land area held by a Native American tribe in the U.S.
Wikipedia

Public Domain Image

The Navajos religious beliefs involve the universe. The universe is a beautiful, ordered and harmonious place. Should this harmony be disturbed or disrupted, then the Navajo religion has rituals to restore this. They use a word *"hozho"* (very difficult to pronounce – like hozy haitch ho) to express this. Harmony and balance is disrupted by death, violence and evil.

Traditional Navajos believe the Diné Bahane' or the *"Navajo creation story"* and *"journey history"* which was given to the Navajo people by the Holy Beings.

Changing Woman is the Holy Being that created the four original clans of the Navajo and saved humans from the monsters that were destroying the earth.

The Navajos believe in two classes of people: **Earth People** and **Holy People**. The Navajo story of creation states that there exists four worlds; three of which are passed through already before making it to the Fourth World (Earth). The fourth and final world is the world in which the Navajo live in now. As Earth People, Navajos must do all they can to maintain balance between Mother Earth and man.

Many prayers for blessings are addressed to **Mother Earth**, **Father Sky**, the **Four Winds** and **White Dawn**. Food and shelter are more than practical objects for the Navajos who are always conscious that they are Mother Earth's gifts.

"The Holy People – First Man, First Woman, Salt Woman and Black God" planned the conditions of life on the surface of the earth. And these four figures are all responsible, not just for the organisation of all things terrestrial, but for the positioning of the stars themselves.

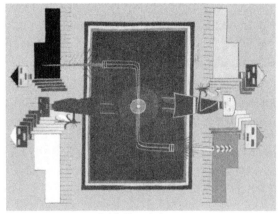

Public Domain Image

The Holy People, or Diyin Diné, had instructed the Earth People to view the four sacred mountains as the boundaries of the homeland (Dinétah) they should never leave:

- Blanca Peak (*Sisnaajiní* — Dawn or **White** Shell Mountain) in Colorado associated with the East
- Mount Taylor (*Tsoodził* — **Blue** Bead or Turquoise Mountain) in New Mexico associated with the South
- San Francisco Peaks (*Dook'o'oosłííd* — **Yellow** - Abalone Shell Mountain) in Arizona associated with the West
- Hesperus Mountain (*Dibé Nitsaa* — **Black** - Big Mountain Sheep) in Colorado associated with the North

Times of day, as well as colours, are used to represent the four sacred mountains.

Wikipedia

For the Navajos, these four colours have special meaning: **black, white, blue** and **yellow**. These colours can symbolize many different things, including spiritual beings and important places in Navajo culture.

The Navajo believe that the Gods pass over the country at dawn. If an individual is up and about he will be blessed by them with health and prosperity. Corn pollen is usually offered to these Gods and for blessings.

Corn pollen is usually carried in a pouch with just a few pinches used to greet the day. Moving clockwise in the four directions.

- East (ha'a'aah) where life began the sunrise.
- South (shadi'dah) is where you get your warmth.
- West (e'e'aah) had to do with the way you spent your day, what was ahead and behind and where the sun set or was 'carried away'.
- North (nahokos) where everything was put to rest.

Corn pollen was collected at harvest-time in September. The women collect the corn and save the pollen by shaking the corn tassels into a container or rubbing with a rag to remove the pollen.

Impurities would be dealt with and the pure pollen would be stored in a jar or a flour sack after being blessed by the medicine man. Only blessed pollen can be used in a medicine bag.

As I am unable to gain copyright for a corn pollen image, the above image is similar.

No two medicine bags are the same because the contents are personal. Even I have one and it's full of items specific to me. It is the same for the Navajo and many other Native American Tribes. It's personal and also individual too.

It's also not a topic for discussion. Navajo rules that just the family might know what was actually in an individual's medicine bag. The Navajo believe that if someone you disliked knew about the contents, then this information could be used to harm you. Beliefs and medicine bags are powerful items.

The medicine bag is the best place to hold your corn pollen, using a small amount to touch your tongue and the top of your head as a morning blessing east, south, west and north.

Navajo families always endeavor to have lots of pollen but ashes would be used if they had run out of pollen itself. Ash, when sprinkled onto an individual may get rid of nightmares or help with their sleep. But traditionally corn pollen was the most popular choice for Navajo beliefs.

The Navajo people cherish their hair as they believe that it is connected to a person's thoughts and therefore should not be cut. The Navajo bun is a traditional hairstyle for both men and women, where their hair is wrapped and then tied with yarn spun from sheep's wool. It looks amazing but I have been unable to gain a picture due to copyright law.

But grieving is different. While grieving the loss of a family member, many tribes do cut their hair. Cutting the hair at these times represents the time spent with the deceased loved one and its ending. But it can also represent a new beginning, or a traumatic life changing event.

Death is obviously a traumatic event for a family, but is handled differently by the Navajo. They believe that when a person dies their body is insignificant and the identity of that person has gone. To ensure that the spirit of that person is released in to the underworld correctly, all ties must be cut.

Navajos believe that an evil spirit or devil (Chinde, pronounced Shin day) is at the bottom of everything that has in any way anything to do with death, and they rarely speak of their dead, for fear of offending the evil spirit; and I have read that the Navajo would rather freeze to death than build a fire out of the logs of a hogan where someone had died. Some

Southwestern tribes, especially the Apache and Navajo, feared the ghosts of the deceased who were believed to resent the living.

CEREMONIES

"A number of healing ceremonies are performed according to a given patient situation. Some chants and rites for curing purposes include:

- **The Blessing Way** *rite is usually done over pregnant women or any person for promoting good health and prosperity. The ceremony is the most frequently used one and resembles how the Holy People acted to create the world and establish harmony.*
- **The Enemy Way** *rite is done as an exorcism to remove ghosts, violence and negativity that can bring disease and do harm to host health and balance.*
- **The Night Way** *is a healing ceremony that takes course over nine days. Each day the patient is cleansed through a varying number of exercises done to attract holiness or repel evil in the form of exorcisms, sweat baths, and sand painting ceremonies. On the final day the one who is sung over inhales the "breath of dawn" and is deemed cured.*

SAND PAINTINGS

Sand painting is the transfer of strength and beauty to the patient through various drawings made by a medicine man in the surrounding sand during a ceremony. Elaborate figures are drawn in the sand using colourful crushed minerals and plants. Many sand paintings contain depictions of spiritual yeii to whom a medicine man will ask to come into the painting in order for patient healing to occur. After each ceremony, the sacred sand painting is destroyed.

Blessing way, **central ceremony of a complex system of Navajo healing ceremonies known as sings, or chants, that are designed to restore equilibrium to the cosmos**. *Anthropologists have grouped these ceremonies into six major divisions: the* **Blessingways, Holyways, Lifeways, Evilways, War Ceremonials** *and* **Gameways**.

But it is the **haatali, or singer**, *who fills the position of medicine man in Navajo culture. Traditionally called a haatali, or "singer", in Navajo, this healer performs ceremonial cures that are targeted at body, mind, and spirit. There are nearly 100 Navajo chants of varying range and intricacy."*
Wikipedia

The number four is sacred to many Native Americans. You may have noticed that the Navajo have four sacred directions, four sacred mountains, four colours and four original clans too. Attempts to create something new is usually unsuccessful the first three times tried. But the fourth time is successful. Four is supposed to be my lucky number too.

Historically, Navajo jewellery is an important part of the Navajo people's cultural heritage. Navajo earrings, necklace and bracelet, are worn to show an individual's cultural identity, status or wealth. They excel in weaving, basket making, pottery making and jewellery with the skill passed onto daughters and granddaughters. All handmade. And it is a very beautiful skill. Certainly well worth wearing if you are lucky enough to own any as the Navajo link turquoise to protection and health.

Public Domain Image

Old and new Navajo bracelets
Silverborders
https://commons.wikimedia.org/wiki/File:Old_and_new_Navajo_brac
elets.jpg
https://creativecommons.org/licenses/by/3.0/legalcode

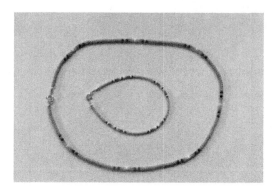

Strangely enough the Navajo culture has the swastika or Whirling Log, as a talisman for well-being, good luck and protection. To us a very odd

11

choice of symbols but the swastika has been used by many cultures for many centuries now, including Buddhism, Jainism and Hinduism — as a symbol of the sun and good fortune.

In the 20th century, traders encouraged Native American artists to use the symbol in their crafts, and it was used by the US Army 45th Infantry Division, an all-Native American division.

The symbol lost popularity in the 1930s due to its associations with Nazi Germany, as it had been suggested that the presence of the swastika across Europe and Asia supported the idea of an ancient Aryan master race (superior specimen of humankind). _{Wikipedia}

In 1940, partially due to government encouragement, community leaders from several different Native American tribes made a statement promising to no longer use the symbol.

A postcard from 1907 showing the Navajo Good Luck symbol

The symbol of **a spiral in a hand** represents the curative powers owned by the Shamans. It brings health and good fortune to those who wear it.

Crossed arrows were symbols of friendship. A broken arrow was a symbol of peace.

But the harmony and balance the Navajo strived for in everything they did was soon to be disrupted and disturbed.

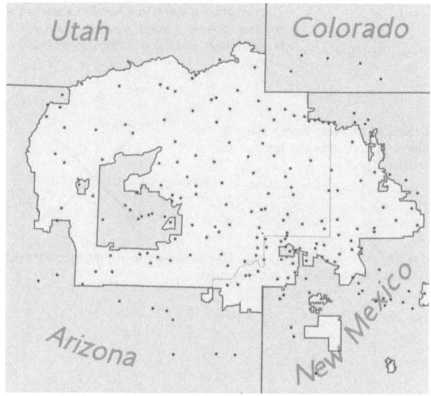

Map showing populated places on the Navajo Nation and surrounding area
Seb az86556 https://commons.wikimedia.org/wiki/File:NavajoNation_map_en.svg
NavajoNation map en
https://creativecommons.org/licenses/by-sa/3.0/legalcode

THE LONG WALK

On May 28th 1830, *'The Indian Removal Act'* was signed into law by United States President Andrew Jackson. This act cleared the land of the Five Civilised tribes, Cherokee, Choctaw, Chickasaw, Creek and Seminole.

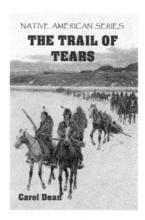

My book *'The Trail of Tears'* explains that these tribes were called *'civilised'* because they had already established farms and cotton farming land, had their own homes, newspaper offices and were living the 'white man's way'. But the white man wanted the land.

This started the *'Trail of Tears'* as it is called by Native Americans and it's described by Wikipedia as *'The Trail of Tears was an ethnic cleansing and forced displacement of approximately 60,000 people of the "Five Civilized Tribes" between 1830 and 1850 by the United States government.'* Wikipedia

Some resisted the sudden removal and were dealt with very swiftly and very deadly.

Many died on this horrendous journey as they were unable to prepare for this journey with adequate food supplies and protective clothing for the cold temperatures they had to endure. Their removal was instantaneous, to get them away from their homes and onto the allocated reservation many miles away.

Many of the five civilised tribes died of cholera, dysentery, measles and smallpox. Others from lack of food or warm clothing. No one knows how many are buried on the trail or even exactly how many survived. But thousands died.

A terrible, terrible time for those involved with devastation effects still felt by those tribes. But it didn't just end there.

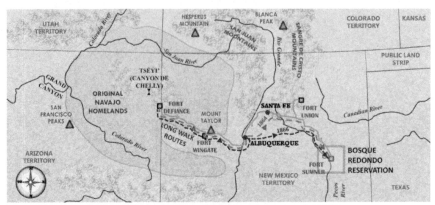

Navajo Long Walks – States as they were in 1866

In the 1860s the Navajo people were the next to face such a trauma. A peaceful people really. Yes they had the occasional conflict with the Spanish, Mexican, Pueblos, Apache, Comanche, Ute, and later European Americans, in order to maintain their ancestral homelands and supplies. So they were used to protecting their sacred lands and were prepared to continue to do so.

Hostilities grew between invading European Americans and Navajo groups over the period of 1846 and 1863. Treaties happened during that time but neither side seemed to stick to it. Raids and skirmishes continued to happen and a disputed horse race led to a huge fight between the Navajo and the US Army. Shots rang out and people on both sides were killed.

An officer, Colonel Chaves, was suspended from duty pending a court martial because of this incident, but charges were subsequently dropped. Eventually General James H. Carelton was appointed in his place as Commander for the New Mexico Military Department in September 1862.

His task was to subdue the Navajos of the region and force them on the long walk to Bosque Redondo Reservation, Fort Sumner, New Mexico. Once appointed he set boundaries to restrict the Navajos from engaging in any sort of conflict. They were not allowed to trespass onto lands, raid neighbouring tribes, or fight with either the Spaniards or European

Americans. Some of the Navajos did agree to these demands but a band of Navajo raiding parties did not. And the whole tribe was penalized because of this.

As the Navajo had not ceded to his demands, Carleton enlisted the help of the famous mountain man Kit Carson. Or should I say, Carleton ordered Colonel Christopher "Kit" Carson to proceed to Navajo territory to receive the Navajo surrender on 20th July 1863.

No Navajos turned up.

Kit Carson and another officer entered Navajo territory to try to persuade the Navajos to surrender. With the help of neighbouring tribes Kit Carson set out to capture as many Navajos as he could in the Navajo territory, or persuade them to surrender. One tribe that proved to be most useful was the Utes. The Utes knew the lands of the Navajo, and were very familiar with Navajo strongholds to.

Kit Carson started a scorched earth policy on the Navajo in January 1864. *'A scorched-earth policy is a military strategy of destroying everything that allows an enemy military force to be able to fight a war, including the deprivation and destruction of water, food, humans, animals, plants and any kind of tools and homes.'* Wikipedia

This scorched earth policy meant that Kit Carson and his men destroyed everything in their path. Navajos were killed, dwellings were burned to the ground, livestock were killed off or captured, irrigated fields destroyed and water sources were fouled, to force those rebellious natives into submission through starvation and desperation. Which they did forcing them to go to Fort Defiance for help.

By early 1864, thousands of Navajo began surrendering and were taken to Fort Canby and those who resisted were murdered. Some Navajos were able to escape Kit Carson's campaign but were soon forced to surrender due to starvation and the freezing temperature of the winter months. Some Navajos refused and scattered to Navajo Mountain, the Grand Canyon, the territory of the Chiricahua Apache, and to parts of Utah. Wikipedia

Public Doman Image

The destruction was senseless and it forced the *Diné* to surrender. They gathered at Fort Defiance and Kit Carson and his troops moved them, on foot, the many, many miles southwest to Bosque Redondo Reservation.

Many Navajo refused to believe that such a terrible thing could happen. Tribal tradition had taught them never to leave their homeland. How could they leave and still be Diné?

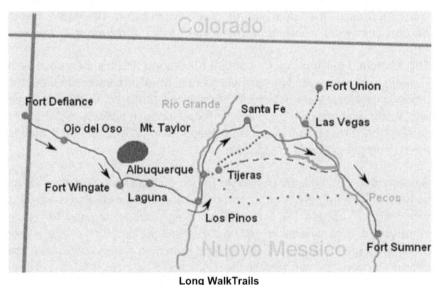

Long WalkTrails
Mario1952 https://commons.wikimedia.org/wiki/File:LongWalkTrails.png
https://creativecommons.org/licenses/by-sa/3.0/legalcode

And it was a non- stop journey. Without much choice left, thousands of Navajo surrendered and were forced to march between 250-450 miles to the Bosque Redondo Reservation.

Between 1864 and 1866, 10,000 Navajo were forcibly removed from their lands to the reservation at Fort Sumner (now in New Mexico) in 53 different forced marches.

The US Government's plan had always been to force the Navajo to adopt the white man's ways. Many Navajo resisted still and swore that they would continue the fight until they were allowed to return to their homelands again. Brave words and feelings. But this did not stop their removal under very dangerous and violent circumstances.

"These soldiers do not have any regard for the women folks. They took unto themselves for wives somebody else's wife, and many times the Navajo man whose wife was being taken tried to ward off the soldiers, but immediately he was shot and killed and they took his wife."
John Daw, testimony before the Land Claims Commission, 1951, cited in *"The Navajo Long Walk"* by Crawford R. Bruell, in *"The Changing Ways of Southwestern Indians: A Historic Perspective"*, ed. Albert Schroeder (Glorieta, NM: Rio Grande Press, 1971), 177.

Navajo people photographed during the Long Walk
Public Doman Image

Navajo leaders – Long walk of the Navajo
Public Doman Image

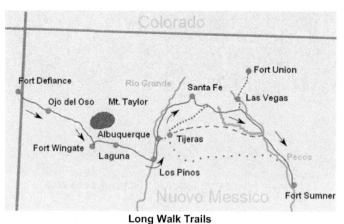

Long Walk Trails
Mario1952 https://commons.wikimedia.org/wiki/File:LongWalkTrails.png
https://creativecommons.org/licenses/by-sa/3.0/legalcode

The Navajo carried what they could, as there were very few wagons or horses to help. They must have felt that their lives were over having to leave their sacred lands as they did. Every long painful step took them further and further away from the land they loved. And the soldiers' orders regarding the Navajo were simple.

If anyone complained of being unwell, kill them.

If someone stopped because they were tired, hungry or thirsty, kill them.

If a woman stopped to give birth to her baby, the soldiers killed her and anyone else who may have stopped to help her. Excerpt from Code Talker by Chester Nez with Judith Schiess Avila

Public Doman Image

Navajo captives at Fort Sumner, c. 1860
Public Doman Image

It soon became apparent to the Diné that they had to do what was necessary to survive as no mercy of any kind was going to be shown them.

Arriving eventually at the Bosque Redondo Reservation they soon discovered there was nowhere to shelter and the ground was not suitable to produce anything as it was very poor. Trying to find any shelter during the winter required digging holes in the earth with *'make do and mend'* lean-tos out of sticks.

Mescalaro Apaches had already been placed at this reservation. The Navajo and Mescalaro Apache had raided each other many a time, so this realisation of sharing a reservation with them caused many a dispute between the tribes.

Bosque Redondo was called a reservation but instead it turned out to be more of an internment camp. They were held there by US soldiers to make sure that they never tried to leave. The original number it was planned to house was 5,000. But already there were 10,000 residing unhappily on the reservation.

Corn crops were tried but failed miserably as the land could not produce a good crop. Plus the Pecos River nearby had a tendency to flood which ruined any chances of anything growing. The Comanche raided the reservation many a time seeking food themselves. Which meant the settlers, also located nearby, had raiding parties from the reservation. They too needed to feed their starving people just trying to survive on the Bosque Redondo replacing what they had lost during the Comanche raids.

Clothing was a problem too. Not just to keep warm but it would have helped. The Navajo tried to make clothes from flour, salt and sugar sacks which were totally inadequate for what was needed. These gave no protection from the cold. But they had to try something to survive.

They were ordered to help build the soldiers barracks which they did, just so that they would be able to exchange some food for their efforts. Food that sadly made them ill. And water was a disturbing challenge as it was very salty and undrinkable for man nor beast. But when that's all you have, then you have to take a chance and drink it.

The Medicine man was unable to help as he would normally have done in their homelands. He must have felt powerless not being able to help his people. He was unable to find the same herbs with which he could heal them and there was no sacred ground to perform the healing ceremonies either. The people felt they were being punished because they had left the Four Scared Mountains. Their homeland. That's why they were so ill and at such **dis-ease**. Plus the US Army were very lax in trying to get the right amount of supplies needed to feed everyone on the reservation. It never worked and there was never enough to go round.

But good news was on the horizon for the Navajo when on 1st June 1868 The Bosque Redondo Treaty was signed and the Navajo Indian Reservation was established.

Food, clothing and an annuity was agreed but the Navajo had to agree to send their children to school for 10 years with the US Government agreeing to establish schools with teachers for every thirty Navajo children. This agreed, the Diné people started to prepare to leave Bosque Redondo properly, for their return home to their lands. But not by the same means as they had arrived. There would be no soldiers to threaten them.

Shortly after the reservation was abandoned as it had turned out to be a disaster.

Marker where the Treaty of 1st June 1868, was signed
Public Domain Image

Manuelito
Public Domain Image

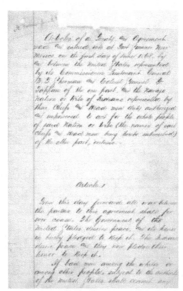

The signers of the document were: W. T. Sherman (Lt. General), S. F. Tappan (Indian Peace Commissioner), Navajos Barboncito (Chief), Armijo, Delgado, Manuelito, Largo, Herrero, Chiquito, Muerte de Hombre, Hombro, Narbono, Narbono Segundo and Ganado Mucho. Those who attested the document included Theo H. Dodd (Indian Agent) and B. S. Roberts (General 3rd Cavalry)

Public Domain Image

It's not very often you will read in Native American history that the US Government gave permission to a tribe to return to their traditional boundaries. In this case the Navajo were granted 3.5 million acres (14,000km) of land inside their four sacred mountains. The Navajo, after the Long Walk, were able to successfully increase the size of their reservation to over 16 million acres (70,000km).

"The Dawes Act of 1887 was designed to divide the communal lands into plots of lands and assigning these to heads of households for their farming. It was introduced to stop tribal land claims and encourage small family farms just as common among the Americans. The land was not considered by the government as reservation land and therefore anything 'left over' when all allotments had been issued meant that the spare land could be sold to non-Native Americans. This land allotment continued until around 1934." Wikipedia

But because of this land being a kind of mixed bag of Native and non-Native reservation land, it is called *'the checkerboard area'*. It also meant the loss of land for the Navajo.

You can imagine, I am sure, the celebrations that were held when they got back to their homelands. Weeks of celebration with many songs, ceremonies of healing and thanksgiving were carried out joyfully.

They had been through terrible, harsh, cruel conditions and forced from their home by the white man. BUT THEY HAD SURVIVED.

Now they could replenish their livestock, plant new crops, and be on their land forever. They were stronger now and more determined to make sure that they would never again be forced to leave the Four Sacred Mountains.

And now the Navajo Nation, also known as Navajoland, is the largest Native American reservation in the United States. As the map shows, from 1868–1934 the land has increased in size. It now occupies portions of north-eastern Arizona, north-western New Mexico, and south-eastern Utah.

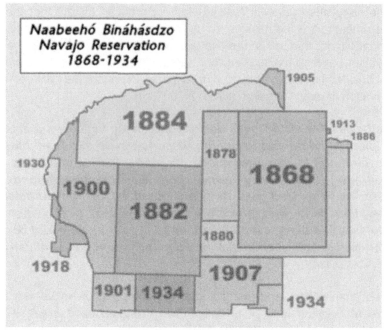

Navajo Reservation 1868-1934
Seb az86556
https://commons.wikimedia.org/wiki/File:Nn_border_hist_map.svg
Nn border hist map
https://creativecommons.org/licenses/by-sa/3.0/legalcode

Long Walk Home, mural by Richard K. Yazzie, 2005
Jay Galvin from Pleasanton, CA, USA https://commons.wikimedia.org/wiki/File:Long_Walk_Home_-
Gallup_Downtown_Murals_-_by_Richard_K_Yazzir,_2005_(16094987121).jpg
Long Walk Home -Gallup Downtown Murals - by Richard K Yazzir, 2005 (16094987121)
https://creativecommons.org/licenses/by/2.0/legalcode

Forever the Diné.

THE BEST TIME OF YOUR LIFE????

Older people often say to the younger members of the family that *'school is the best time of your life'*. There are many of the Native American families who could argue that point, as school was rather more severe than just compulsory as it was for us.

The idea of schooling was fairly simple really as far as the US Government was concerned. The schools were there to encourage the Native American children to reject their own culture and traditions in favour of the white man's ways.

It was felt that it was *"cheaper to educate them than to fight them"*. The US Government's words, not mine.

What the school founders actually meant was, that the schools were there to eliminate the children from the ways and life they had known, and to assimilate them into the white man's world. Whether they liked it or not!

In order to do this the best plan that they could come up with was to literally take children away from their families to be in their schools.

Public Domain Image

Some Native American children as young as 5 years old were taken from their homes and had severe punishments inflicted on them for speaking their native language. In this case, Navajo. Nothing from their home was allowed – not even the smallest piece of jewellery.

When the new 'students' arrived at the school, there was a complete disregard for their feelings, or any form of kindness or understanding. The teachers had no knowledge of what these children's beliefs were, or what their life was about, nor did any of the teachers try to find out. It was a military style regime, and most of the staff were military personnel anyway, so it was very strict.

And the first thing they did to welcome their new 'students' to the school was to cut their hair short (a source of shame for boys of many tribes), put the children into uniforms (which meant that their normal clothes were destroyed) and they were then forced to give up their meaningful names and pick an English name. Very hard to do when you have no understanding of the language or what it means, so names were more than likely picked for them.

The children were humiliated and made to feel that their cultures and traditions were inferior and they were often ridiculed and taught to be ashamed of the life they once knew and loved. Tribal songs were banned as was anything remotely ceremonial, particularly if it involved wearing 'savage' clothing. Some children managed to hold onto their own clothing, but the bulk of it would have been destroyed as soon as they arrived. The only clothing allowed was the white man's clothing in the form of the school uniform.

It was more like a prison camp than school. Children used to whisper to each other in Navajo but only if they knew they would not be found out. Being classed as savages anyway they needed the discipline. And they got it readily. Forced to sit up straight with your arms folded in front of you as stiff as statues.

Speaking in their native tongue was a punishable offence. The children were not even allowed to speak to one another in their own language, only English. If they were caught talking to each other in their native language, then punishment was swift and hard, given a beating with sticks, rulers or belts. Because you had to learn that the white man's way was the right way. And you would be punished until you did.

Children had **"their mouths washed out with lye soap when they spoke their native languages; they could be locked up in the guardhouse with only bread and water for other rule violations; and**

they faced corporal punishment and other rigid discipline on a daily basis. Wikipedia

English was the only language to be spoken and for someone who had not heard the language used nor attempted to use it, school times were a dangerous nightmare. With the words YES and NO written on the blackboard the pupil then had to try and pick the correct answer from whatever the teachers question was. An impossible task when you don't understand what is being said to you.

Picking a response from the blackboard could lead to severe punishment if you chose the wrong one. Some were brave enough to try, but I fear many would rather stay quiet than get punished yet again.

Again if you needed the bathroom you had to ask in English. Get it wrong or not know the English words, then it was a long time until the class finished.

They had to forget their cultures – traditions, or else – because it was spawned from the devil.

Some tried to run away but they were always brought back by the Navajo police. Usually because the escapees had gone home so they were easy to find. But once back to school, they would be punished yet again – but undeterred they would try to get away many times.

And this treatment catered for all Native American children.

Christianity was forced onto them too, as they had to attend church services always under duress. Religion should be a personal choice but they had none.

The government felt that their Navajo charges at Fort Defiance, the school location, should be Christian. Catholic actually. Their traditions, their beliefs, their ceremonies had to be forgotten. They were taught about the birth of Jesus, about Christmas and surprisingly enough it was actually celebrated at the school. Navajo children would receive candy and fruit and a tree would be erected and decorated as per the season. Never seen before by the Navajo.

Fort Defiance, Arizona
Public Domain Image

This new religion, I feel, confused them even more, as the Navajo way stresses the importance of a balanced life. Respecting all things in nature even the rocks, trees and grass. The Catholic Church taught them to be in awe of God's creation of the world but no affinity with nature at all. They found this most confusing and I would imagine they had many upsetting times trying to decide where they belonged – here with the white man's Catholic faith or back on the reservation with their own beliefs?

All Navajo ceremonies and beliefs were looked upon as pagan rites by the teachers and clerics at school. Their Gods were false Gods and they had no problems drumming this home to the Navajo children there. The Navajo way was wrong as far as the white man was concerned and similarly the Navajo looked upon the white man's religion as wrong too. It's hardly surprising there was confusion.

Navajo medicine man Nesjaja Hatali, 1907
Public Domain Image

Having said all that the children were given lessons in maths, science and they were taught trades and practical skills (agriculture, carpentry, printing, art, music and drawing). I would imagine, and I could be wrong, but I think that these lessons will have been 'drummed' into them forcibly. Some may have enjoyed this new learning admittedly, but there are good ways to teach children. Ways that they can look back on and possibly gain an interest or enjoyment out of a particular topic. But again there would be no choice. They were there to learn and it didn't matter how it was done.

Hopefully the skills and knowledge that they eventually gained, compensated them for the harsh method of learning. Many of the Native American children did go onward and upward despite their initial educational experiences thankfully.

Public Domain Image

Then when your 'stint' at school was over, the truck driver would drop the Navajo children nowhere near where they lived and they had to walk perhaps three to four days before they reached their home. Contact with your family to say you were on your way home was impossible, as there was no contact allowed with their family on the reservation. Many of these youngsters would be about 8 years old, if that.

But for some, the education gained did prove useful and they and their language became indispensable to the white man not all that long after this.

THE STOCK REDUCTION PROGRAM

But way before all this, the Spanish had introduced churro sheep to the Navajo during the 1540s, gaining the sheep through trade or raid from settlers.

Navajo Churro Sheep
Just chaos
https://commons.wikimedia.org/wiki/File:Navajo_Churro_Sheep.jpg
https://creativecommons.org/licenses/by/2.0/legalcode

The sheep had a significant effect on Navajo life and transformed them from a nomadic hunter and gatherer culture, to one of farming and herding. Over the years the herds grew tremendously. They were important to the Navajo culture and a huge source of prestige and admiration.

Public Domain Image

By the 1930s the US Government, through the Bureau of Indian Affairs (BIA), brought in a policy to reduce the large Navajo herds, stating that an acre of land could only support six sheep.

BIA agencies held meetings with Navajo men telling them how many sheep the land would support. Why the agencies met with the Navajo men is not known, since by tradition, the sheep belonged to the Navajo women.

1930 brought surprise and distress to the Navajo People when the BIA suddenly sent bulldozers onto their land. Without any real explanation the bulldozers proceeded to dig trenches about 150 feet long and about five feet deep. On all the neighbouring land too.

Days later the BIA men returned and told the Navajo to round up their sheep and goats and herd them into the trenches. Protesting was futile. They would be jailed if they did not comply. Reluctantly the animals were herded into the pits and the pits sealed, then these live animals were sprayed with paraffin and set on fire.

The noise, the smell, the screams of the animals, let alone the distress of the Navajo must have been horrendous. It had taken years for many of them to establish their farms working hard to make it work. Having healthy animals was a good sign and sheep were a measure of success. Now all that work and effort had literally just gone up in smoke.

Many farms suffered the same fate. Anything over a hundred head of sheep was open to 'reduction'. Horses and cattle were killed to but they were shot where they stood.

Initially, the Navajo were paid for their sheep, as the government slaughtered them, but as the reductions went on, sheep, goats and horses they were simply shot and their carcasses left to rot in the fields.

In all, the federal agents killed more than 250,000 sheep and goats and more than 10,000 horses belonging to the Navajo people. The Stock Reduction Program caused starvation on the Navajo Reservation.

When new breeds of sheep were introduced to the Reservation they were unable to thrive in the severe habitat and the quantity of their wool was not sufficient for Navajo weaving.

Public Domain Image

Finally during the 1970s animals with the characteristics of the old churras were gathered and the Navajo-Churra Sheep Project founded. The breed has been saved from extinction and is again gaining in popularity.

A WAY TO WIN THE WAR?

It wasn't long after the Stock Reduction Program and the atrocities of Pearl Harbour, Hawaii on 7th December 1941, that an ancient people committed themselves to helping '*Nahasdzáán*', Mother Earth and the United States by serving in the Marines.

The beginning of another story in the lives of the Navajo and a very important and brave one.

News of the Japanese attack came reaching the Navajo Nation via the radio. The United States had entered into World War II.

The Diné men began to enlist even though some of them were really underage for this. Their hard living circumstances on the land, plus their military style schooling at the 'white man's' boarding schools had already given them the 'true grit' to face the rigours of a soldier's life.

For some, it would come as an ironic turn of events, as the boarding schools had punished severely if they spoke their language. Now the whole train of thought had changed. It was needed as you will soon find out.

And this is how I understand the American/Japanese war. A very difficult and complex subject, and you will find that I have not attempted to describe actual fighting, battle tactics, or commands given/received. I am, however, not taking the subject lightly. I am telling it my way and I have written about the heroism, but also the malaria, dysentery and the dangerous and desperate conditions.

But I am also not forgetting the constant danger they were encountering. The trauma of it all will have been unbearable. A dreadful time for all, but they all, Native American and non-Native American, still have to be admired for enduring this for their fellow man, their country and the world. Bearing up through lack of food, medicine, dry clothing and always facing the physical stress of it all. They are to be admired and honoured for their bravery. Hopefully now you understand. Here goes.

Japan is an island country consisting of a string of islands in East Asia. The Japanese had been allies of the United States and Britain in WWI, and had prospered greatly through their expanding trade and soon had a reputation as a political and economic force in eastern Asia.

But the Japanese population was increasing and the need to feed and provide for its people became increasingly challenging. Because of this and as its own finite resources being inadequate for this task, it looked outwards seeking to satisfy these increasing demands. But also to satisfy Japan's imperial ambitions to build an empire within Eastern Asia.

With these imperial ambitions in mind they turned their attentions towards their neighbour, China, a land of untold riches and opportunities. Invasion plans started to form. Plans of conquest to take by force, if needed, all the resources that were required.

In order to obtain these vital resources the conquest was started in 1931 when they invaded Manchuria, Northern China, with its rich fertile resources.

Taking over the Chinese import market would also help. They began by invading China near Beijing then Shanghai in 1937, and Nanking in December with thousands of Chinese people massacred.

By September 1939, World War II had started with Great Britain and France declaring war on Germany. Japan already had a Tripartite Pact with Germany and Italy. This pact created a defence alliance between the three countries and was intended to stop the United States from joining the conflict of WW II.

The **Tripartite Pact**, also known as the **Berlin Pact**, was an agreement between Germany, Italy and Japan signed in Berlin on 27th September 1940. Japan recognized *"the leadership of Germany and Italy in the establishment of a new order in Europe." In return, Germany and Italy recognized Japan's right to establish a new order "in Greater East Asia."*
Wikipedia

The purpose of the Pact, directed against an unnamed power presumed to be the United States, was to **deter that power from supporting Britain**, thereby not only strengthening Germany's and Italy's cause in the North African Campaign and the Mediterranean theatre, but also weakening British colonies in South-East Asia.

In August 1941, because of the increased aggressive moves from Japan into Southern Indochina, America retaliated by freezing Japanese assets stopping them from buying oil and also stopped shipping goods to them. Goods that were vital because it was more of an underdeveloped country and they couldn't get the goods themselves. America stepped in with political trade restrictions to try and restore peace and security again through embargoes and economic sanctions. For those of you who don't understand.

An **EMBARGO** stops trade between countries. This means that the countries in question will get poorer. The hope is that the problem within the country will stop. Wikipedia

A **SANCTION** is a threatened penalty for disobeying a law or a rule. Wikipedia

Specifically, the oil embargo organised by America with the British and the Dutch, as Japan imported about 90% of its oil. Without the oil Japan and their military would grind to a halt and their thoughts of war would have to diminish. America froze all Japanese assets in the US preventing Japan from purchasing oil.

Unwilling to agree to US demands Japan decided to take the oil they needed by force by attacking British Malaya and the Dutch East Indies because of its oil fields. A commodity Japan really needed.

Attacking Pearl Harbour first became a priority. As war was now inevitable, Japan's only chance was to surprise and destroy America's navy.

Attacks were planned by the Japanese, one being Pearl Harbour. Japan intended the attack as a preventive action to stop the United States Pacific Fleet from interfering with its planned military actions in Southeast Asia against overseas territories of the United Kingdom, the Netherlands, and those of the United States.

President Roosevelt had already ordered the US Pacific Fleet from California to Pearl Harbour in 1939. Pearl Harbour was a huge oil and fuelling station for US ships and planes which the Japanese decided that a successful attack there would cripple the US military and stop them in their tracks. On 7th December 1941 Japan attacked Pearl Harbour.

"The attack killed 2,403 U.S. personnel, including 68 civilians, and destroyed or damaged 19 U.S. Navy ships, including 8 battleships. The three aircraft carriers of the U.S. Pacific Fleet were out to sea on manoeuvres." Wikipedia

"But, the result of the attack did not enable Japan to expand in the Pacific. It did not result in the acquisition of more natural resources. And, the restrictions were not lifted as a result of the attack."
Wikipedia

While America was still reeling from the surprise attack at Pearl Harbour, Japan continued with simultaneous attacks on British forces in Malaya, Singapore and Hong Kong, among others, beginning World War II in the Pacific conquering British Malaya and the Dutch East Indies and gaining the resources needed to continue the fight.

Other attacks were Guadalcanal, Midway Islands and the Philippines.

After Pearl Harbour, war was declared against Japan on 8th December 1941 by the United States. And more men were needed to help win the fight.

Once the word got out, many Navajo turned up to enlist.

"We are doing our best to win the war to be free from danger as much as the white man. We are fighting with Uncle Sam's army to defend the right of our people to live or own life in our own way."
Quote from Lewis Naranjo (Santa Clara Pueblo) Wikipedia

And they did enlist in huge numbers after the attack on Pearl Harbour in 1941. About 44,000 Native Americans saw active duty including around 800 women. They too needed to protect their country. Not just the United States, but their ancestral homes too.

The problem was, the Navajo didn't have a birth certificate system within the people. No one was really sure how old they actually were. It was a guessing game and a lot of the Navajo guessed themselves older so that they could enlist without any queries.

This had now become a personal fight for their lands, their traditions. They were joining the fight for the **preservation of their lands rather than the United States**.

There were many Protection Way Ceremonies to ensure that the individual enlisting was protected doing the specific tasks expected of him by the Marines. There were protection songs with an arrowhead (blessed) or a talisman with some meaning for the individual to carry and protect him. Along with his medicine bag and the corn pollen they carried for blessings each day by putting pollen of their tongue to talks to spirits and pollen on their head to think or plan.

Once enlisted, the huge step was leaving the reservation, their families, their friends, their way of life and facing literally the unknown.

They were initially sent to California to a boot camp. Literally a crash course to see if they could become fighters along with their US counterparts. Well we are talking Navajo here and these guys were very strong men. Their lives as sheep farmers working the Navajo land, had hardened them from an early age. The early starts mentioned in boot camp was no challenge at all as they were used to this tending the sheep. Really they already had a head start on many of the recruits at camp.

They were also expected to undergo arduous training sessions carrying packs, running on very rough terrain and going without food and water for some time. Things that you and I would perhaps not wish to endure and certainly not be able to do. Or at least I know I couldn't. But it was a piece of cake to the Navajo.

The conditions they had to live and work with on their sacred lands had built up a huge resistance to this kind of endurance. They didn't notice any real discomfort. It seemed from what I have read, very easy for them to master. They were very advanced, strong men and their progress through the various Marine trials was classed as highly satisfactory.

Sgt L. J. Stephenson said of the Navajo *"Magnificent specimen of 'original American' manhood they are already farther advanced than recruits usually are"*. Excerpt from; Code Talker: The First and Only Memoir by One of the Original Navajo Code Talkers of WWII

While the training progressed the Japanese continued to try to continue forward in their plan to destroy anything and everything American. They thought they had the perfect battle tactics and were winning through deciphering any coded transmissions the US were sending. Being able to do this gave them the upper hand.

The US needed a code that could not be deciphered by the Japanese and they needed it quickly.

In WWI the Comanche and Choctaw had been utilised to use their language and it had been a success. Again strange for the US to suddenly need the Native Americans to speak their own language when it had been barred and punishments were very severe if you did use your language in the white man's schools. But the Comanche and Choctaw had made a success of it.

But after the war it is said that the Germans discovered which of the native languages had been used in the codes, and sent people into those tribes as a kind of spies, pretending to be someone else (tourist, teacher) and learning the language firsthand. The Navajo had not been utilised during the First World War and the language had no English influences to mar it.

The idea to use Navajo for secure communications came from a man called Philip Johnston, the son of a missionary to the Navajos. He had lived among them since being a young child on the reservation, and one of the few non-Navajos who spoke their language fluently, and learnt their customs.

Johnston was also a World War I veteran and knew that the military were still looking for an unbreakable code. Realising that Native Americans had been used successfully in the First World War, as signalmen, he felt that as the Navajo language was so complex, it could fox the Japanese totally.

The US Marines and Navy along with the US Army, needed something to help them and suddenly the Native American language was again a good idea. Johnston knew of the military's need to send and receive messages with an unbreakable code.

He took his idea to the Naval Office in Los Angeles and they liked what they heard and Johnston was sent on meet with Major Jones and Major General Clayton B. Vogel USMC (United States Marine Corp). He was able to explain how he felt the Navajo people and their language, could help. This he confirmed, by speaking Navajo to Major Jones, completely confusing him.

But Johnston's proposal also stated that the fluency of reading Navajo could only be accomplished by ***"individuals who are first highly educated in English, and who, in turn, have made a profound study of Navajo, both in spoken and written form"***. Excerpt from https://www.archives.gov/publications/prologue/2001/winter/navajo-code-talkers.html

That it was not a language that could be readily understood or learnt without actually being a Navajo. Because of this Johnston felt that the Navajo were the best candidates to recruit for a role such as this. The boarding schools attended by the Navajo for years, had drilled into them the English vocabulary giving them the necessary requirements for military service and to transmit messages in their native language.

The Navajo, like other Native Americans, were born to the warrior tradition. The Navajo saw themselves as inseparable from the earth they lived upon, protectors of anything sacred to the people and this intense feeling drove them to defend the land.

And this is exactly what the marine recruiters were asking the Navajo to do. Make a difference in the home of the white man. This could change their lives forever. Or finish their lives completely. Scary stuff.

General Vogel had a telephone connection set up between two offices and had written six typical military messages out to send. One said, *"Enemy expected to make tank and dive bomber attack at dawn."*

Normally messages were sent in English, (it was called a Shackle Code) encoded via the coding machine and sent. At the receiving end the message was de-coded and written in English. This took quite some time. Sometimes about an hour.

A shackle code is a cryptographic system used in radio communications on the battle field by the US military. It is specialized for the transmission of numerals. Each of the letters of the English alphabet were assigned a numeric value. A number could have several letters assigned. The assignation was changed frequently and required the distribution of the codes to each party in advance. When a party wanted to communicate a number, it radioed "SHACKLE" and it spelled out each digit (or combination of digits) using a word starting with the letter. The end of the number was marked by the word "UNSHACKLE". Wikipedia

When the Navajo were given the same message to transmit and receive it only took 40 seconds. And the information de-coded was correct.

After much investigation, and hearing the language, the US thought that perhaps it could work. Not definitely, but it could work. But there was a long way to go.

After viewing a demonstration of messages sent in the Navajo language, the Marine Corps was so impressed that they recruited 29 Navajos in two weeks to develop a code within their language. Although at the time General Vogel did request a further 200 Navajo. His selling pitch in a way was quite complimentary as he reported that the Navajo dialect was *'completely unintelligible'* to other tribes making it impossible to decipher. He had to make do with 29 to start with.

But they still had to meet the requirements needed for anyone enlisting and take on the same training as any other recruit. Plus the strict English/Navajo language requirements.

On 5th May 1942 the first 29 Navajo arrived at San Diego, California, for basic training in military and weapons use. This lasted seven weeks before they transferred to Camp Elliot for courses in message transmission and radio operations.

Then the really big day arrived when they were taken to one side, secretly, and asked if they could come up with an unbreakable code. But they had to be proficient in English and Navajo. And they were tested to ensure that they were not just saying that they were.

But the Navajo language is very complex. It has to be heard to be understood and that's by a very trained ear among the Navajo themselves. Words used can and do have a differing meaning which we know, but in Navajo the words reflect how various objects interact.

Saying something like you have to 'pick something up' really depends on what it was you were actually picking up. It depends on the shape and consistency of the item being picked up. If it's a stick or a bucket or a sandwich, then the verb that would need to be used would be completely different or it would not make sense.

There are also various tones used when speaking the language. This again can completely change the meaning of the words if the correct tone is not used. Sorry but I can't give you examples of this as there is no way that I could even attempt to try. My research has reinforced this, as have Navajo themselves, how complex it is and I believe them.

One translation I can give you from a book called 'Code Talker' by Chester Nez with Judith Schiess Avila is as follows;

The speech does not state simple facts; it paints pictures. Spoken in Navajo the phrase *"I am hungry"* becomes *"Hunger is hurting me"*. Sounds so much nicer.

But all the same, to suddenly have the mammoth task of designing an unbreakable code to be used during wartime must have been a daunting prospect. Being told that this was not something you could discuss or disclose to anyone would be hard too. That they would be unable to communicate with anyone outside as this project was so secret.

Navajo families ties are strong and not knowing where your loved one was or what they may be facing must have been unspeakably hard for the Navajo to agree too. Their families would not know what they were doing and the Navajo were told never to go anywhere on their own unless they were in pairs. Not even to the loo.

But the fact that ties were strong between the Navajo meant that similar ties would be just as strong throughout the 29 in the group too.

Once the instructor was satisfied that they understood the implications of it all and agreed to the terms, he told them what they were expected to do.

They had to design a complex code using a word for each letter of the alphabet. The code eventually contained about 450 phonetically spelt words and then had to be memorised. Each letter of the alphabet had to consist of one to three Navajo names or short words to spell out the information in a message. Once this was done they had to memorise it so that they would be proficient with each other and that all knew and understood this particular code. And then locked in a room together to achieve this.

The code was so complex once devised, it meant that even members of the Navajo Nation themselves would not be able to decipher the code, even though they too spoke Navajo. The only people to understand and work the code were the Navajo code talkers themselves. And it had to be top secret which means just that. *TOP SECRET*.

Coding came in two different types in World War II.

TYPE ONE was based on 26 Navajo terms that meant individual English letters of the alphabet had a Navajo equivalent. Such as Navajo for 'ant' is 'wol-la-chee'. This word became the word for the letter A in English.

TYPE TWO were words translated straight from English into Navajo. The Navajo developed a dictionary of 211 terms (expanded later to 411) for military words. Words that did not exist, in the Navajo language. If there was no word in their language to fit the military word, they would find one in perhaps a phrase. Navajo did not have **submarine** in their language so they substituted it for **iron fish**.

To make sure that each one of the code talkers had memorised the code they would test themselves as often as possible throwing in words to make it harder, but always getting it right. They devised, as part of the task, phonetic English spellings for unwritten Navajo words. These became part of the new code as it all had to be perfect and easily transmitted in the throes of battle.

And of course their writing had to spot on too. It had to be legible and it was decided all written in upper case and it all had to look the same too.

As a team they were very quick really which surprised the US. It took them about five days to come up with Navajo word equivalent for the full alphabet. The most difficult letters were J and Z. Jackass chosen for J and Zinc chosen for Z.

The code talkers learnt quickly. As they had memorised everything and were fluent in converting the code from memory to each other at a very fast rate, despite the pressure they were under to achieve this. As a group they were determined that this was going to work. They knew it could and they knew that working together and supporting each other, it would be a success.

English messages needed to be encrypted orally into Navajo and sent via radio. When the message was received, it would again be orally decrypted from Navajo into written English. Sounds an OK plan but in the heat of battle with the world exploding around you? Bit of a different story?

Determined not to fail the Navajo code talkers continued to study and study hard.

But there were military terms needed to be coded too. Various officer ranks Navajo equivalents had to be found plus names for boats, planes and military equipment. Three new Navajo were pulled away from duty to assist with this, Felix Yazzie, Ross Haskie and Wilson Price. Their help became invaluable to this task and they too fought alongside in the battles ahead.

- Names for a fighter plane became *da-he-tih-hi* or hummingbird

- A battleship was *lo-tso* or whale

- A destroyer was *ca-lo* or a shark

Using animal names worked.

- A bomb was *a-ye-shi* or eggs

- A hand grenade was *nimasi* or potato

- Japan was *beh-na-ali-tsosie* or slant eye

All this and more including the months of the year, names of the US companies fighting and every scrap of military equipment now catered for within the Navajo code.

To test them out, they were given messages to code and decode. The US made sure that the Navajo receiving the message could not see the Navajo sending the message. Just in-case there were some kind of signals that made the code easier to interpret.

During one trial of a practice code the Navajo were told it would take about 4 hours for this particular message to be de-coded. The Navajo sent it and it was de-coded on 20 seconds. The US could not believe this could be right and tested them on many differing messages only to discover the same result. IT WORKED.

The Navajo language, although looking like an alien language, was fast becoming a God send to the US military.

Messages were coded and de-coded and the code talkers just got better and better at what they did.

Subsequently a code book was devised to teach new potential Navajo code talkers all the relevant words/phrases etc. If you were not trained in this code, even though you might speak Navajo fluently, you would not understand any messages sent. And this code book was only for training purposes and never left base to be taken into battle. It was all memorised.

Now was the time to try out this theory for real. And they were deployed to South Pacific.

I have to say that I found this part of my research really surprising. I had this picture of the code talker sitting somewhere in the US or in a small hideaway room in safety away from the dreadful goings on with the battle with the Japanese. I was so wrong.

Public Domain Image

These guys were right in the thick of it. They were deployed in pairs. One to work the equipment, and one to send/receive messages in their language and translate into English. Many times right on the beach where the fighting was occurring. Highly dangerous and they were always a favoured target for the Japanese, as they targeted officers, medics, and radiomen. Meaning the code talkers had to try and keep moving as soon as they had transmitted their messages.

And I suppose if you think about it seriously, they would need to be right there to ensure that messages were dealt with as quickly as possible. But the conditions were horrendous.

Code talker on Tarawa, November 1943
USMC Archives from Quantico, USA
https://commons.wikimedia.org/wiki/File:Code_talker_on_Tarawa,_November_1943_(7973459298).jpg
Code talker on Tarawa, November 1943 (7973459298)
https://creativecommons.org/licenses/by/2.0/legalcode

It turned out that there were between 375 and 420 Navajo code talkers who additionally joined the US fight serving in every assault that the US were involved with during the second world war. By April 1943 a further 200 code talkers had finished their training and the original recruits were attached to marine divisions in the South Pacific. But there was still a shortage of available code talkers. Many battalions and regiments had to manage without their expertise.

The code was so successful that Philip Johnston re-enlisted as Staff Sergeant and began training code talkers in November 1942. He continued this role for the remainder of the war with Navajo code talkers being passed onto him once they had passed their basic training.

Military terminology proved a bit of a problem to the Navajo and the Navajo had to adapt their language to a phonetic code with other vocabulary adaptions to meet those military needs through warfare messages.

Giving airplanes names after birds – buzzard is a bomber – hawk a dive bomber and using clan names for divisions, battalions and regiments aided this adaption.

FURTHER EXAMPLES OF NAVAJO CODE

English Letter	Navajo Word	Meaning
A	Wol-la-chee	Ant
B	Shush	Bear
C	Moasi	Cat
D	Be	Deer
E	Dzeh	Elk
F	Ma-e	Fox
G	Klizzie	Goat
H	Lin	Horse
I	Tkin	Ice
J	Tkele-cho-gi	Jackass
K	Klizzie-yazzie	Kid
L	Dibeh-yazzie	Lamb
M	Na-as-tso-si	Mouse
N	Nesh-chee	Nut
O	Ne-ahs-jah	Owl
P	Bi-so-dih	Pig
Q	Ca-yeilth	Quiver
R	Gah	Rabbit
S	Dibeh	Sheep
T	Than-zie	Turkey
U	No-da-ih	Ute
V	A-keh-di-glini	Victor
W	Gloe-ih	Weasel
X	Al-an-as-dzoh	Cross
Y	Tsah-as-zih	Yucca
Z	Besh-do-gliz	Zinc

English Word	Navajo Word	Meaning
Corps	Din-neh-ih	Clan
Switchboard	Ya-ih-e-tih-ih	Central
Dive Bomber	Gini	Chicken Hawk
Torpedo Plane	Tas-chizzie	Swallow
Observation Plane	Me-as-jah	Owl
Fighter plane	Da-he-tih-hi	Humming Bird
Bomber	Jay-sho	Buzzard
Alaska	Beh-hga	With-Winter
America	Ne-he-Mah	Our Mother
Australia	Cha-yes-desi	Rolled Hat
Germany	Besh-be-cha-he	Iron Hat
Philippines	Ke-yah-da-na-lhe	Floating Land

Iwo Jima was a battle that is mentioned many times I discovered during my research. Heading there to code talk will have been a first flight for many a Navajo. In military planes too, perhaps not the best way for your first experience of flight. Very scary, yes, with many prayers to the Great Spirit for a safe landing.

The Japanese held Guadalcanal and as a fighting force, they were trained never to surrender. They followed the Bushido code which was an *'ancient way of the warrior'* developed by the samurai. This meant a fight to the death killing as many enemy as you could while doing it. Some chose to blow themselves up, definitely taking many of the enemy with them at the time. Anything really, as surrender was a non-starter, They had to die for the Emperor which was expected of them and an honourable way to die for them too.

"They were indoctrinated from an early age to revere the Emperor as a living deity, and to see war as an act that could purify the self, the nation, and ultimately the whole world."
https://www2.gvsu.edu/walll/Japan NO SURRENDER.htm

"The tradition of death instead of defeat, capture, and shame was deeply entrenched in Japanese military culture; one of the primary values in the samurai life and the Bushido code was loyalty and honor until death." Wikipedia

Within this framework, the supreme sacrifice of life itself was regarded as the purest of accomplishments.

The US had their own Manifest Destiny many years ago and Japan had theirs too. This taught them that all eight corners of the world would one day be under one roof – through the control of Japan's emperor.

In the eyes of the Japanese, the American soldiers were weak and not willing, like them, to die for their country. The US soldiers were strong fighters, even when the odds seemed against them. But they knew that, although being captured by the Japanese meant that they would be treated very cruelly, this did not mean they would be dishonoured by the US military on their return, should they live through capture. Whereas the Japanese would rather die than be captured by the enemy, as surrender is a sign of cowardice. That's how they achieved honour. So therefore the American soldiers were classed as weak.

**Japanese control of the western Pacific area between May and August 1942.
Guadalcanal is located in the lower right centre of the map**
Public Domain Image

The battle for Guadalcanal was a long and hard three day battle. Aircraft from Henderson Field destroyed four Japanese transporter ships and the US began to take over the Pacific. Eventually the Japanese started to withdraw from Guadalcanal and many headed for the mountains, which became a stronghold for them. But the battle continued.

United States Marines rest in the field during the Guadalcanal campaign
Public Domain Image

51

Henderson Field
Public Domain Image

Exhaustion would set in quickly and be seen on the faces of the marines. But relief had been promised and it seemed like a long time coming. Sadly the relief was not to be for the code talkers. They were doing too valuable a job to be allowed to go.

Public Domain Image

But being some of the first onto the beaches, the code talkers distinguished themselves as warriors very early on. Brave just being there, although fully qualified in battle order, as all the US Marines were still a scary place to be when you're face to face with it all. If they needed to protect themselves from the Japanese they were fully skilled to do so. Not a problem there. But it wasn't just the Japanese they had to worry about.

They had to dig themselves into the sand to try and gain some cover and protection from snipers to start with, digging themselves into a fox hole. This is where they would begin sending their messages from. But what they didn't realise was, they were not alone.

It wasn't just protecting yourself from the Japanese. There were huge crabs that came out at night, and their bodies were as big as your hand, then add legs and claws on top of that. They were blue, black or red-orange in colour and ugly to boot and they came out to eat from the dead bodies of soldiers on the beach, or to attack anyone in the vicinity.

Crab
U.S. Fish and Wildlife Service Headquarters https://commons.wikimedia.org/wiki/...
...File:Palmyra_Atoll_National_Wildlife_RefugePacific_Islands_(6109853163).jpg
Palmyra Atoll National Wildlife Refuge, Pacific Islands (6109853163)
https://creativecommons.org/licenses/by/2.0/legalcode

They had violent tendencies and could take a finger off easily with a snip or snap of their claws. They lived in the sand during the day, so depending on where you had dug yourselves in, come night time there might be more than just the two Navajo in the dug-out. Very scary.

Flares would be set off occasionally to see if there were any Japanese soldiers around the Marines fox holes. Instead it would show the many thousands of those crabs scuttling about the sand looking for food.

And you have to realise that the code talkers could not disclose their position by suddenly jumping up in fright or trying to run away. Japanese snipers were everywhere. There was no lighting up a cigarette or even trying to relieve yourself. Any kind of movement would alert the enemy very quickly.

The Navajo tell a story of one code talker (Harry Tsosie) who crawled out of his foxhole and stood up to relieve himself in the dark only to be shot by a US navy medic. It wasn't until the next morning it was discovered who had been shot. The medic had no idea what had happened either until morning. Tsosie was a friend too many code talkers and one of the first code talkers to die. Friendly fire it's called and although the US medic will have suffered terrible trauma due to this dreadful accident, a lesson was learnt the hard way.

Public Domain Image

But they had also been warned about the crocodiles that surfaced at night. They could be heard near-by as they apparently made very strange noises, dry like a purr or really noisy like an engine. So yes they could be heard, but they could not be seen. Sometimes the crocodiles tried to climb into the fox holes. Not what you want as your trying so hard not to be seen.

Crocodile
AngMoKio
https://commons.wikimedia.org/wiki/File:Crocodile_Crocodylus-porosus_amk2.jpg
Crocodile Crocodylus-porosus amk2
https://creativecommons.org/licenses/by-sa/2.5/legalcode

Public Domain Image

Once given a message to code and send the code talker immediately had to move their position as the Japanese were skilled at picking up transmission signals and blowing up the area it came from. Code talkers had to be fast movers that is for sure.

Code talkers at work

Oft times the message couldn't get through via the normal process and code talkers had to run the gauntlet over hostile ground to get the message through. Sometimes 400-500 yards to run which will have seemed like miles under those circumstances, zig zagging across sand hoping that you're not mistaken for a Japanese suicide soldier.

There were a few reports of Navajo being mistaken for Japanese even if they were wearing the uniform of the marines. It would be assumed that they had stolen the uniform from a dead US marine. Standing up to armed US marines must have been quite daunting but the Navajo had to stand their ground and try to explain. It was only through their persistence that an officer would be called quickly to verify their reason for them being there. They could not say that they were code talkers. This was still very hush hush.

But perhaps to the naked ear, the Navajo language may have sounded somewhat foreign or even perhaps Japanese. Although nothing like it. And many had decided that the Navajo did have a Japanese look about them. That wouldn't help either.

But the name Navajo or Indian had to remain unspoken by the marines. No one wanted the Japanese to cotton on to any dangerous conclusions. 'Chief' was then decided upon as a name and it stuck.

As the code talkers had become rather indispensable to the US, they were assigned bodyguards. Even though they may have been 'buddies' beforehand, their 'buddies' were now there to make sure that code talkers were kept safe.

In various documents and info, it is apparently stated that the rules the bodyguards had to follow were if a code talker was killed then the blame fell squarely on the shoulders of the bodyguard who had to explain what had happened. They were told to stay alert, and if they needed a break someone else had to take their place.

But the worrying thing for the code talkers was, if they were in potential danger of being captured by the Japanese, did their marine 'buddies' have orders to kill them? Knowing that the Japanese army tended towards torturing their captives, being shot may have felt like a better way to go. But no 'buddie' was put in that position thankfully, which must have been a relief all round.

The following story emphasises the reason behind the marine 'buddie'.

A Navajo man named Joe Kieyoomia (Key–oh- me) joined the Army in 1941 happy to fight for the country he belonged to. He was part of the Bataan Peninsula and captured by the Japanese after the Pearl Harbour attack, joining the horrendous (Bataan Death March).

"During the march, prisoners received little food or water, and many died. They were subjected to severe physical abuse, including beatings and torture. On the march, the "sun treatment" was a common form of torture. Prisoners were forced to sit in sweltering direct sunlight without helmets or other head coverings. Anyone who asked for water was shot dead. Some men were told to strip naked or sit within sight of fresh, cool water. Trucks drove over some of those who fell or succumbed to fatigue, and "cleanup crews" killed those too weak to continue, though trucks picked up some of those too fatigued to go on. Prisoners were randomly stabbed with bayonets or beaten." Wikipedia

Initially tortured because his captors thought he was Japanese-American (and therefore a traitor), Kieyoomia suffered months of harsher punishment and beatings before the Japanese accepted his claim to Navajo ancestry.

He survived the Death March that killed thousands of starving US and Philippine soldiers. When the "Navajo Code" had the Japanese baffled, Kieyoomia was questioned and tortured although, as he was deployed to the Philippines with New Mexico's 200th Coast Artillery, he didn't even know about the existence of the code, he could only understand bits and pieces of what the Navajo Code Talkers were saying. But they soon twigged that Joe might just be able to help then decipher the American transmissions. So far they had been very unsuccessful.

Eventually, this led him to tell the Japanese that it sounded like nonsense to him.

As punishment for his inability to crack the code and possibly because the Japanese viewed him as unwilling to crack the code, he was stripped naked and forced to stand for hours in deep snow until he talked. When he was finally allowed to return to his cell, a guard shoved him, causing the soles of his feet to tear as they were frozen to the ground.

After surviving the prison camps, the "hell ships" and the torture, Kieyoomia was a prisoner in Nagasaki when that city was the target of the second atomic bomb dropped by the US Army Air Forces (USAAF). Kieyoomia survived the attack, saying he was protected by the concrete walls of his cell.

"After 3½ years as a prisoner of war, he was abandoned in the city for three days after the bombing, but says a Japanese officer finally freed him." Excerpt from https://en.wikipedia.org/wiki/Joe_Kieyoomia

Joe was one of the lucky ones, I guess. He was a POW for 1,240 days moving from camp to camp and finally arriving in Japan. Joe felt that they thought that he too was of Japanese ancestry by his surname as this sounded slightly Japanese. That he had just strayed from the path and perhaps they could make him return to his true people. The Japanese.

He was eventually rescued after the Japanese surrendered and his extensive wounds and physical conditions took a long while to repair. But Joe had no knowledge of the code talkers code. It was a code within a code and he would have had to have all the training before he could possibly have been able to decipher it. He was just one man and the Japanese would have had to have captured many very cooperative code talkers to be able to crack the code. They would never have allowed this to happen as a result of their commitment to total secrecy.

But Joe's ordeal was looked on by the Navajo as a kind of blessing. Sounds weird, but he was tortured but kept alive by the Japanese just in-case he could crack the code. The code was there to save lives. In a way it had saved his.

And the code talkers were held in very high regard and the effectiveness of the code shone through. Major Howard Connor, signal officer of the 5th Marine Division at Iwo Jima said, *"During the first 48 hours, while we were landing and consolidating our shore positions, I had six Navajo radio nets operating around the clock. In that period alone, they sent and received over 800 messages without error."*
Excerpt from Navajo Weapon by Sally McClain

Navajo code talkers spent much time stuck in foxholes for hours and hours on end, with no way to remove the pungent odour they developed on their body and clothing, never mind all the dead soldiers left there. With the tremendous heat on the island this encouraged flies and maggots in their thousands to arrive. Bodies decomposed very quickly in those hot steamy conditions. But the flies didn't restrict themselves to the soldiers. They attacked anyone that may have had an open wound.

The hardships continued. It seemed as though there was no 'let-up' from combat situations. The Japanese were relentless in their attacks but at Bougainville the battle decimated the Japanese. More than one thousand Americans and seven thousand Japanese died at Bougainville.

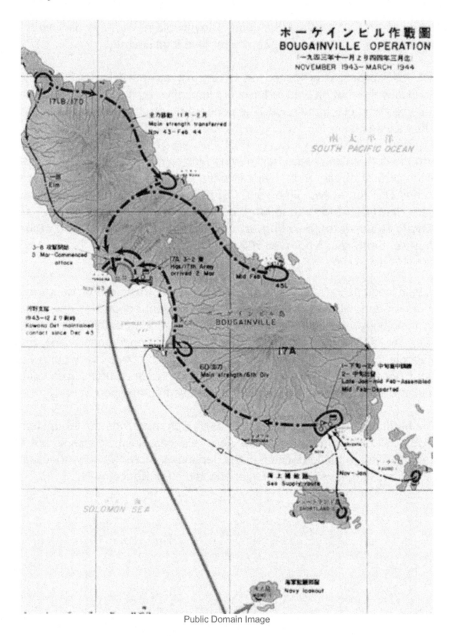

Public Domain Image

But being posted there meant a little reprieve for the 3rd Marine Division and the code talkers stationed there, as they could take advantage of clean clothes, a haircut and good food thanks to the Naval Construction Battalions (Seabees). The Seabees built airfields, hospitals anything that was needed and they didn't mind sharing their rations with their fellow marines.

Code talkers on Bougainville, 1943
USMC Archives from Quantico, USA
https://commons.wikimedia.org/wiki/File:Code_talkers_on_Bougainville,_1943_(7973456676).jpg
Code talkers on Bougainville, 1943 (7973456676) https://creativecommons.org/licenses/by/2.0/legalcode

3rd Marine Division, 2nd Raider's sign on Bougainville
Public Domain Image

If not with the Seabees, then your helmet rinsed out and used over a small camp stove to cook their meals. No large fires though. A give away for the Japanese to take pot shots at you.

Image by Pexels from Pixabay

The messages sent and received were coded and de-coded in record time making the taking of Iwo Jima a success. The US could not have had such success if it had not been for the Navajo code talkers. The whole code totally baffled the Japanese and they could not crack it no matter how hard and how long they tried. Even though they tried extremely hard to disrupt messages by trying to jam the radios or shout, sing, anything that may put the code talkers off what they were doing. It never worked though. The code talkers were too professional and too used to each other that the confidence shone through and the Japanese were ignored.

Despite the hardships and the danger, Marines had landed on Iwo Jima on 19th February 1945. Major Howard Connor, 5th Division signal officer, said that without his code talkers the island would not have been taken.

Many have said that they *"were worth their weight in gold"*, *"thoroughly professional"*, *"their contribution in the South Pacific probably immeasurable"*, *"courageous facing dangerous situations"*.

A member of the Marine Special Forces group stated in *'Code Talker'* by Chester Nez with Judith Schiess Avila, *"Most Marines and Army personnel never had a clue what the 'coders' were and what major part they played in our war. If God alone may know, they saved thousands of American lives, yet their tale has been hidden by the very role they played."*

Many battles were fought and won with the code talkers volunteering to go to the front. Code talkers served in all six US Divisions during the conflicts. Thirteen code talkers died during the battles and many witnessed multiple deaths on both sides. And the Navajo have a tradition regarding the dead

"The Navajo also buried their dead quickly with little ceremony. Any Navajos exposed to a corpse had to undergo a long and costly ritual purification treatment. For the Navajo, it is important to live in hohzo, a state of order with the universe which recognizes the beauty of all living things." Wikipedia

When their part of the war was over, the code talkers were returned to their reservation. There was no ticker tape parades waiting for them or any of their fellow marines returning home. The war was still raging when some came home.

Germany surrendered in May 1945 but Japan continued to fight. The Allies knew that something had to be done. And it was.

Hiroshima was targeted with atomic bombs on August 6th 1945, followed closely with Nagasaki on 9th August 1945. Further bombs, not atomic, were dropped on Tokyo 13th August 1945 causing massive devastation. The Japanese surrendered.

After the atomic bombs American troops were sent in to study the devastation caused. It had never been studied and all their observations of the impact caused, was transmitted through the Navajo code to the US. They needed to know:

- What vegetation was left?

- How many had died from the impact?

- Were people still dying?

What a dreadful job but the information was reported back using the code and Navajo code talkers. But it was over.

Quite a few Navajo were eventually sent back home after they had the usual recourse of the discharge process. Towns and cities celebrated the return of their sons, brothers, husbands and fathers. And it was a time to celebrate. But not all were included in those celebrations.

After being held in quarantine for a couple of weeks discharge papers were issued, base pay and mileage given and you had to find your own way back home after that.

And on their return home, the Navajo code talkers were given strict instructions not to mention anything that they had done particularly with the code. They realised that this was going to be very hard not being able to speak about their experiences with their families.

Letters to and from their families during the war had already had very severe censoring by the US. Hardly worth reading as the bulk of each letter was blacked out.

But their families would want to know what they had done and where they had been too. It was going to be very hard for the Navajo.

No recognition came from the US. They wanted everything to remain hushed up and secret in case the code would be needed again. So no medals and no ticker tape parades. Not like their US counterparts who were greeted warmly and loudly by Americans everywhere else.

Navajo people had no celebrations for their returning people. It's not how they would deal with things. They are a very quiet, modest people and although they respected the fact that individuals had joined in the battle to help protect their land and their people, it was really what was expected of them. The returning Navajo understood this.

They had no attention and no benefits from joining in and fighting alongside their American brothers. But the Navajo still had the trauma of it all, although there were support groups to try and help them release any feelings and help them to cope with the trauma. But not for the Navajo. Talking about this was again something they could not do. They had been told not to talk about their role in the war, so therefore they could not have this support. They could not open up and talk freely about the role they had played and the impact of it all.

These were really cases of PTSD, *(post-traumatic stress disorder (PTSD) is a mental health condition that's triggered by a terrifying event — either experiencing it or witnessing it. Symptoms may include flashbacks, nightmares and severe anxiety, as well as uncontrollable thoughts about the event)* long before this was actually accepted and dealt with as a serious condition within the military. The term 'shell shock' was given after WWI which has the same symptoms as

PTSD. But it was 1980 before this condition was recognised.
https://www.mayoclinic.org/diseases-conditions/post-traumatic-stress-disorder/symptoms-causes/syc-20355967

But they did have their traditions and ceremonies of their own.

Navajo believe that if someone kills another it means that their spirit follows that someone. And it haunts them knowing this after what they had witnessed and the amounts of people killed.

Many tried to come to terms with this fear/worry/nightmares until it got just too much to bear for some and an Enemy War Ceremony was often performed to cleanse the warrior returning from battle from the taint of the enemy's spirit. And this tradition would help the individual to repair themselves after such trauma. A Purification Ceremony or a Squaw Dance Ceremony could assist this too bringing peace of mind again.

Many Navajo decided that the experience they had had with the Marine Corps was a good one and stayed on becoming 'twenty year' men, joining different areas of the service and fighting in Korea.

Some applied to colleges and universities to finish their education as part of the Servicemen's Readjustment Act 1944 (G.I. Bill.) Training gave them the opportunity to train as engineers, teachers, mechanics and ranchers to mention a few. Becoming part of the tribal government, shaping the policies that the Navajo Nation still enforces to this day.

But not everyone was that fortunate as many code talkers felt that the respect given to them by their fellow American Marines would be exactly the same within the 'white world'. But it was almost impossible to find work and this led to drinking problems which led to lack of self respect and problems both mental and physical.

But secrecy had to be maintained. And the Navajo did. Despite their dreadful circumstances. Until 1968 when the code was de-classified. Once the Navajo people realised what their family members had gone through during the war itself, there were a few local ceremonies and the code talkers could proudly wear their special uniforms.

HONOURS

We honour the generations that have come before and we are mindful of those yet to come

From 1969, after declassification of the code happened, recognition began albeit in a small way. Although funds had to be raised to have a silver medallion made to present to the code talkers. Although I am unable to gain copyright to use an image of the silver medallion itself.

The medallion was inspired by a rather nice painting by Joe Ruiz Grandee of Ira Hayes. *"Ira Hamilton Hayes was an Akimel O'odham Native American and a United States Marine during World War II. Hayes was an enrolled member of the Gila River Indian Community, located in Pinal and Maricopa counties in Arizona."* Wikipedia

I am unable to gain copyright to reproduce an image of the painting, but it is described as *"Hayes is dressed in hunting regalia of the Pima tribe and sitting astride an Indian pony. In the mist in the background if the famous image of the second flag raising on Iwo Jima."* Excerpt from Navajo Weapon by Sally McClain

Seventh War Loan Drive Poster (May 11–July 4, 1945)
Public Domain Image

Ira Hayes
Public Domain Image

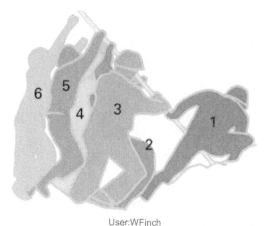

Raising the Flag
The six second flag-raisers:
1 Cpl. Harlon Block (KIA)
2 Pfc. Harold Keller
3 Pfc. Franklin Sousley (KIA)
4 Sgt. Michael Strank (KIA)
5 Pfc. Harold Schultz
6 Pfc. Ira Hayes

Wikipedia

Cpl. - Corporal
Pfc. - Private First Class
Sgt. - Sergeant

KIA - Killed in Action

User:WFinch
https://commons.wikimedia.org/wiki/File:Raising-the-Flag.jpg
Raising-the-Flag
https://creativecommons.org/licenses/by-sa/3.0/legalcode

After they had gained permission to use the imagery, the medallions were minted and ready to present to Navajo code talkers representing many of the US Divisions during WWII.

An NBC programme called 'Real People' in 1981 mentioned a small part of the role of the code talkers during WW II. Many people watching this programme were inspired enough to write to the President to try and gain some recognition for the work the code talkers had achieved. President Reagan issued a certificate of recognition to the code talkers and made 14th August 1982 as Navajo Talkers Day.

Various forms of recognition happened in the next few years including museum displays in the Pentagon.

"The 'Honoring the Code Talkers Act', was introduced by Senator Jeff Bingaman from New Mexico in April 2000 and made law on December 21, 2000. This new law called for recognition of the Navajo code talkers. The act authorized the President of the United States, President Bill Clinton, to award the Congressional Gold Medal, to the original twenty-nine Navajo code talkers as well as silver medals to each man who later qualified as a Navajo code talker (about 300).

The medals were awarded during a ceremony in the Rotunda of the U.S. Capitol on July 26, 2001, where large number of members of the Navajo nation, both veterans and their families and friends, attended the ceremony.

Many of the Navajo Code Talkers receiving medals wore their Navajo Code Talkers Association regalia. Five of the original twenty-nine were still alive, and four attended the ceremony: Allen June, Lloyd Oliver, Chester Nez, and John Brown, Jr.

Family members represented those who could not be present, and they held pictures of those family code talkers." Excerpt from https://www.archives.gov/publications/prologue/2001/winter/navajo-code-talkers.html

Navajo code talker uniform
HaeB
https://commons.wikimedia.org/wiki/File:Navajo_code_talker_uniform.jpg
https://creativecommons.org/licenses/by-sa/3.0/legalcode

From my research I have discovered that a moving and motivational speech came from a Sergeant Major of the Marine Corps, Alford McMichael. The crowd attending were inspired to greet his final very appropriate words by giving him a standing ovation when he said ***"Semper Fidelis code talkers! Semper Fidelis my fellow Marines! Semper Fidelis my fellow Americans."*** Meaning ***"Always Faithful"*** the motto of the Marines.

Excerpt from https://www.archives.gov/publications/prologue/2001/winter/navajo-code-talkers.html

President George W. Bush also made a moving speech after which he presented gold and silver medals to those alive and to the families of the missing friends. 29 Navajo were honoured. Recognition had taken a long time coming but a very proud moment for those receiving medals and all the families attending. The victory had been shared and now they shared the history of it all with their American brothers.

"Today, America honors 21 Native Americans who, in a desperate hour, gave their country a service only they could give. In war, using their native language, they relayed secret messages that turned the

course of battle. At home, they carried for decades the secret of their own heroism. Today, we give these exceptional Marines the recognition they earned so long ago

The gentlemen with us, John Brown, Chester Nez, Lloyd Oliver, Allen Dale June and Joe Palmer, represented by his son Kermit, are the last of the original Navajo Code Talkers. In presenting gold medals to each of them, the Congress recognizes their individual service, bravely offered and flawlessly performed.

With silver medals, we also honor the dozens more who served later, with the same courage and distinction. And with all these honors, America pays tribute to the tradition and community that produced such men, the great Navajo Nation. The paintings in this rotunda tell of America and its rise as a nation. Among them are images of the first Europeans to reach the coast, and the first explorer to come upon the Mississippi.

But before all these firsts on this continent, there were the first people. They are depicted in the background, as if extras in the story. Yet, their own presence here in America predates all human record. Before others arrived, the story was theirs alone.

Today we mark a moment of shared history and shared victory. We recall a story that all Americans can celebrate, and every American should know. It is a story of ancient people, called to serve in a modern war. It is a story of one unbreakable oral code of the Second World War, messages traveling by field radio on Iwo Jima in the very language heard across the Colorado plateau centuries ago.

Above all, it's a story of young Navajos who brought honor to their nation and victory to their country. Some of the Code Talkers were very young, like Albert Smith, who joined the Marines at 15. In order to enlist, he said, I had to advance my age a little bit. At least one code talker was over-age, so he claimed to be younger in order to serve. On active duty, their value was so great, and their order so sensitive, that they were closely guarded. By war's end, some 400 Navajos had served as Code Talkers. Thirteen were killed in action, and their names, too, are on today's roll of honor.

Regardless of circumstances, regardless of history, they came forward to serve America. The Navajo code itself provides a part of the reason. Late in his life, Albert Smith explained, the code word for America was, "Our Mother." Our Mother stood for freedom, our religion, our ways of life, and that's why we went in. The Code Talkers joined 44,000 Native Americans who wore the uniform in World War II. More than 12,000 Native Americans fought in World War I. Thousands more served in Korea, Vietnam and serve to this very day.

Twenty-four Native Americans have earned the highest military distinction of all, the Medal of Honor, including Ernest Childers, who was my guest at the White House last week. In all these wars and conflicts, Native Americans have served with the modesty and strength and quiet valor their tradition has always inspired.

That tradition found full expression in the Code Talkers, in those absent, and in those with us today. Gentlemen, your service inspires the respect and admiration of all Americans, and our gratitude is expressed for all time, in the medals it is now my honor to present.

May God bless you all."

President George Bush's speech
https://georgewbush-whitehouse.archives.gov/news/releases/2001/07/20010726-5.html

After his speech, President Bush presented the gold medals, sharing a moment with each of the veterans.

Bill Toledo, Robert Walley and Alfred Newman
Public Domain Image

President Bush also passed a law in 2008, The Code Talkers Recognition Act of 2008 on 15th November recognising every Native American Code Talker who had served during WWI and WWII with a Congressional Gold Medal. Some Navajo were the exceptions from this as they had already been awarded this medal previously.

In 2008 the Navajo Nation also erected a memorial to the code talkers in Window Rock, Arizona, the capital of the Navajo Nation.

Navajo Code Talker Memorial
John Fowler https://commons.wikimedia.org/wiki/File:Navajo_Code_Talker_Memorial.jpg
https://creativecommons.org/licenses/by/2.0/legalcode

Each year now the Navajo have the Annual Navajo Parade of the Code Talkers where they proudly wear their code talker uniforms, celebrate their time together and the experiences they shared too. And sadly the numbers are dwindling due to the age of many of them now.

'The memorial park has many symbolic structures: a statue of a Navajo Code Talker with his 32 pound radio (Westinghouse – Type CRI-43007 transmitter) on his back, a circular path outlining the four cardinal directions (East = White; South = Blue; West = Yellow and North = Black), 16 angled steel pillars with a sign filled with names of war veterans, a healing sanctuary that is used for reflection and solitude that features a fountain made of sandstone' Wikipedia

Navajo Nation World War II Memorial (Names)
Ngmweb https://commons.wikimedia.org/wiki/File:Navajo_Nation_World_War_II_Memorial_(Names).jpg
https://creativecommons.org/licenses/by-sa/3.0/legalcode

Visitors can pay their respects to all those code talkers involved.

The Navajo ensure that the language is continually taught in schools with highly trained Navajo language teachers instructing in the language and a further set of teachers instructing in the English language too. Right from kindergarten onwards.

29 CODE TALKERS

Charlie Y. Begay **PURPLE HEART**
Roy L. Begay
Samuel H. Begay
John Ashi Benally
Wilsie H. Bitsie
Cosey S. Brown
John Brown, Jr.
John Chee
Benjamin Cleveland **PURPLE HEART**
Eugene R. Crawford
David Curley
Lowell S. Damon
George H. Dennison
James Dixon
Carl N. Gorman
Oscar B. Ilthma **PURPLE HEART**
Alan Dale June
Alfred Leonard
Johnny R. Manuelito
William McCabe **PURPLE HEART**
Chester Nez
Jack Nez
Lloyd Oliver
Joe Palmer
Frank Denny Pete **PURPLE HEART**
Nelson S. Thompson **PURPLE HEART**
Harry Tsosie **PURPLE HEART KIA**
John Willie
William Dean Wilson

**Chester Nez is the last survivor of the original
WW2 Navajo code talkers – he died in 2014**

Public Domain Image

Chester Nez
Public Domain Image

The Purple Heart is a United States military decoration awarded in the name of the president to those wounded or killed while serving, on or after 5th April 1917, with the US military. Wikipedia

Peter MacDonald
CPM2021
https://commons.wikimedia.org/...
...wiki/File:Peter_MacDonald
Sr._Navajo_Code_Talker_World_War_II.jpg
https://creativecommons.org/licenses/...
...by-sa/4.0/legalcode

Thomas H. Begay
Richard Ricciardi
https://commons.wikimedia.org/wiki/...
...File:Thomas_H_Begay.jpg
https://creativecommons.org/licenses/by/...
...2.0/legalcode

I was unable to find a copyright free image of John Kinsel Snr. but in 2023 it was reported that John Kinsel Snr., Peter Macdonald and Thomas H. Begay were the only three code talkers still alive.

Finding work after the war proved to be very hard. Although well respected for their part in the war, this respect was not the same back in 'white society'.

Lack of respect, no job, no way to support yourself, or your family leads to many problems – alcohol being one of them. Losing your self respect and heading down that slippery slope with alcohol is not a good path to follow. But even at their lowest state, the code talkers did not reveal their secret.

Code Talkers Monument in Ocala, Florida Memorial Park
Mlpearc https://commons.wikimedia.org/wiki/...
...File:Code_Talkers_Monument_in_Ocala,_Florida_Memorial_Park.jpg
https://creativecommons.org/licenses/by-sa/3.0/legalcode

HAGONEE

 But times change. Or do they?

The Navajo are still living on their sacred lands but living is a very loose term to use. Many don't have electricity or water and are still trying to eke out a living farming sheep on this desert of land they love so much.

Unemployment is six times the average for America and getting worse. They are literally struggling to live from day to day. Still classing themselves as prisoners of WW II. How sad.

Thankfully the land they live on is the most visited, the most photographed, and the most popular of sights to see in America. Everyone wants to go there and thankfully many film moguls still feel that this is the area to film in.

Arguably one of the greatest classic Westerns of all time, John Ford's *"The Searchers"* was shot in Monument Valley along with his *"Cheyenne Autumn"*, *"She Wore a Yellow Ribbon"* and others. *"The Searchers"* is the one to see. Many films were made there, in addition to TV shows, including *"City Slickers"*.

"Forrest Gump" — the 1994 Oscar-winning movie of the same name starring Tom Hanks — who had ran for three years, two months, 14 days, and 16 hours when he reached the hill that looks toward Monument Valley Navajo Tribal Park, where he *"put the past behind him and moved on"*.

Other list of projects in Monument Valley include titles like *"2001: A Space Odyssey"*, *"Indiana Jones and the Last Crusade"*, and *"Back to the Future Part III"*. To be honest, turn on many a cowboy film, even these days, and you will see a part of Monument Valley there. But there are so many films that it's just impossible to mention them all. I told you it was a popular place.

Only three remaining members are still living as of 2023, **John Kinsel Snr.**, **Thomas H. Begay**, and **Peter MacDonald**. Some Code Talkers such as **Chester Nez** and **William Dean Yazzie (aka Dean Wilson)** continued to serve in the Marine Corps through the Korean War. Approximately 461 Navajo Marines served as code talkers, with 13 killed in action although I'm only able to find 11 names.

The Totem Pole inside Lower Monument Valley is an incredible and remarkable rock feature. It is the tallest spire in the world at a prominence of 381 feet and total height of 400 ft. **Bill Feuerer**, **Jerry Gallwas**, **Mark Powell** and **Don Wilson** were the first to climb the Totem Pole on 11th – 13th June 1957.

Monument Valley Totem Pole
Anonymous https://commons.wikimedia.org/wiki/File:Monument_Valley_Totem_Pole.jpg
https://creativecommons.org/licenses/by-sa/3.0/legalcode

And part of the Windows in Arches National Park holds a tribute to all the Navajo Code Talkers and is quite a sight to see.

Navajo Code Talker Memorial
John Fowler https://commons.wikimedia.org/wiki/File:Navajo_Code_Talker_Memorial.jpg
https://creativecommons.org/licenses/by/2.0/legalcode

Visiting it, as we did just recently in 2023, you can understand the Navajo having this special bond with the land. It's huge, it's magnificent and if you have read any of my other Native American Series of books you will also understand my fascination and need to see this land for myself. Mother Earth did a beautiful job in Monument Valley and even this 'white woman' could feel a deep spiritual feeling just by being there.

My heart has always wanted me to go there. I felt like I was being called to this beautiful area, and I felt good and proud to have been able to walk the land of the Navajo ancestors. The land healed me too.

The Navajo people have no word for goodbye. In our language, **"goodbye"** means gone and physically separated and that's it, they're not with you anymore as they have left. It might be that they have left after a visit, or they are off back to their home or going on a holiday. It's just a temporary separation. They will be back.

In Navajo language it agrees that there is a physical parting, but it also means they have not really left us because the *'imprints of their character remain on us.'* They are remembered basically which is a nice way to look at it.

Instead they say *"hagonee"* (pronounced: Hah-go-neh) which means something like, *"be well until I see you again".*

And that's my wish for you too. I hope you have enjoyed reading about the Navajo Nation and their Code Talkers and until the next time,

HAGONEE

CODE TALKERS LIST

Akee, Don
Alfred, Johnnie
Allen, Perry
Anderson, Edward B.
Anthony, Franklin A.
Apache, Jimmie
Arviso, Bennie
Ashley, Regis
Attikai, Harold
Augustine, John
Ayze, Lewis F.
Bahe, Henry Jr.
Bahe, Woody
Baldwin, Benjamin C.
Barber, William
Beard, Harold
Becenti, Ned D.
Becenti, Roy Lewis
Bedoni, Sidney
Begay, Carlos
Begay, Charlie Sosie
Begay, Charlie V.
Begay, E.
Begay, George K.
Begay, Henry
Begay, Jerry C. Sr.
Begay, Jimmie M.
Begay, Joe N.
Begay, Lee
Begay, Leo
Begay, Leonard
Begay, Notah
Begay, Paul (KIA)
Begay, Roy
Begay, Samuel H.
Begay, Thomas H.
Begay, Walter
Begay, Willie Keskoli
Begay, Wilson J.
Begaye, Fleming D. Sr.

Begody, David M.
Begody, Roger
Belinda, Wilmer
Belone, Harry Sr.
Benally, Harrison Lee
Benally, Harry
Benally, Jimmie L.
Benally, John Ashi
Benally, Johnson Delwashie
Benally, Samuel
Bennallie, Jimmie D.
Benton, Willie Sr.
Bernard, John
Betone, Lloyd
Bia, Andrew
Billey, Wilfred E.
Billie, Ben
Billiman, Howard Jr.
Billison, Samuel
Billy, Sam Jones
Bitse, Peter John
Bitsie, Wilsie H.
Bitsoi, Delford E.
Bizard, Jesse J.
Black, Jesse
Blatchford, Paul H.
Bluehorse, David
Bowman, John Henry
Bowman, Robert
Brown, Arthur C.
Brown, Clarence Paul
Brown, Cosey Stanley
Brown, John Jr.
Brown, N.A.
Brown, Tsosie Herman
Brown, William Tully
Buck, Wilford
Burke, Bobby
Burnie, Jose Jr.
Burnside, Francis A.
Burr, Sandy
Cadman, William
Calleditto, Andrew

Carroll, Oscar Tsosie
Cattle Chaser, Dennis
Cayedito, Del
Cayedito, Ralph
Charley, Carson Bahe
Charlie, Sam Sr.
Chase, Frederick
Chavez, George Sr.
Chee, Guy Claus
Chee, John
Clah, Stewart
Clark, Jimmie
Claw, Thomas
Cleveland, Benjamin
Cleveland, Billie
Cleveland, Ned
Cody, Leslie
Cohoe, James Charles
Craig, Bob Etsitty
Crawford, Eugene Roanhorse
Crawford, Karl Kee
Cronemeyer, Walter
Crosby, Billy
Curley, David
Curley, Rueben
Dale, Ray
Damon, Anson Chandler
Damon, Lowell Smith
Davis, Tully
Deel, Martin Dale
Dehiya, Dan
Dennison, George H.
Dennison, Leo
Dixon, James
Dodge, Jerome Cody
Dooley, Richard
Doolie, John
Doolie, Richardson
Draper, Nelson
Draper, Teddy Sr.
Etsicitty, Kee
Etsitty, Deswood
Evans, Harold

Foghorn, Ray
Foster, Harold V.
Fowler, King
Francisco, Jimmy
Freeman, Edwin
Gatewood, Joseph P.
George, William
Gishal, Milton M.
Gleason, Jimmie
Goldtooth, Emmett
Goodluck, John V.
Gorman, Carl Nelson
Gorman, Tom
Gray, Harvey
Grayson, Bill Lewis
Greymountain, Yazzie
Guerito, Billy Lewis
Gustine, Tully
Guy, Charles
Harding, Ben Williams
Harding, Jack W.
Hardy, Tom
Harrison, Emmett
Haskie, Ross
Hawthorne, Roy
Haycock, Bud
Hemstreet, Leslie
Henry, Albert
Henry, Edmund Juan Sr.
Henry, Kent Carl
Hickman, Dean J.
Holiday, Calvin
Holiday, Samuel T.
Housewood, Johnson (KIA)
Housteen, Dennle
Howard, Ambrose
Hubbard, Arthur Jose
Hudson, Lewey
Hunter, Tom
Ilthma, Oscar B.
Jake, H.
James, Benjamin
James, Billy

James, George B.
Jenson, Nevy
Johle, Elliott
John, Charlie T.
John, Leroy
Johnny, Earl
Johnson, Deswood R.
Johnson, Francis T.
Johnson, Johnnie
Johnson, Peter-WIA
Johnson, Ralph
Jones, Jack
Jones, Tom H.
Jordan, David
Jose, Teddy
June, Allen Dale
June, Floyd
Kearns, Percy
Keedah, Wilson
Kellwood, Joe H.
Kescoli, Alonzo
Ketchum, Bahe
Kien, William
King, Jimmie Kelly Sr.(KIA)
Kinlahcheeny, Paul(KIA)
Kinsel, John, Sr.
Kirk, George H. Sr.
Kirk, Leo(KIA)
Kiyaani, Mike
Kontz, Rex T.
Lapahie, Harrison Sr.
Largo, James
Leonard, Alfred
Leroy, George
Leuppe, Edward
Little, Keith M.
Lopez, Tommy
MacDonald, Peter
Malone, Max
Malone, Rex
Malone, Robert
Maloney, James
Maloney, Paul E.

Manuelito, Ben Charlie
Manuelito, James Sr.
Manuelito, Johnny R.
Manuelito, Peter R.
Manuellto, Ira
Marianito, Frank
Mark, Robert
Martin, Matthew
Martinez, Jose
McCabe, William
McCraith, Archibald
Mike, King Paul
Miles, General
Moffitt, Tom Clah
Morgan, Herbert
Morgan, Jack C.
Morgan, Ralph (KIA)
Morgan, Sam
Morris, Joe
Moss, George Alfred
Multine, Oscar P.
Murphy, Calvin Henderson
Nagurski, Alolph N.
Nahkai, James T. Jr.
Nakaidinae, Peter
Napa, Martin
Naswood, Johnson
Negale, Harding
Newman, Alfred K. Sr.
Nez, Arthur
Nez, Chester
Nez, Freeland
Nez, Howard H. Sr.
Nez, Isreal Hosteen
Nez, Jack
Nez, Sidney
Notah, Ray
Notah, Roy
Notah, Willie A.(KIA)
Odell, Billy
Oliver, Lloyd
Oliver, Willard V.
Otero, Tom

Paddock, Layton Sr.
Pahe, Robert D.
Parrish, Paul A.
Patrick, Amos Roy
Patterson, David E.
Peaches, Alfred James
Peshiakai, Sam
Pete, Frank Danny
Petterson, Joe Sr.
Pinto, Guy
Pinto, John
Platero, Richard
Preston, Jimmie
Price, Joe Frederick
Price, Wilson H.
Reed, Sam
Roanhorse, Harry C.
Sage, Andy
Sage, Denny
Salabiye, Jerry E. Sr.
Sandoval, Merril L.
Sandoval, Peter P.
Sandoval, Samuel
Sandoval, Thomas
Scott, John
Sells, John C.
Shields, Freddie
Shorty, Dooley
Shorty, Robert T.
Silversmith, Joe A.
Silversmith, Sammy
Singer, Oscar Jones
Singer, Richard
Singer, Tom (KIA)
Skeet, Wilson C.
Slinky, Richard T.
Slivers, Albert James
Slowtalker, Balmer
Smiley, Arcenio
Smith, Albert
Smith, Enock
Smith, George
Smith, Raymond R.

Smith, Samuel Jesse Sr.
Soce, George Bill
Sorrell, Benjamin G. Sr.
Spencer, Harry
Tabaha, Johnie Sr.
Tah, Alfred
Tah, Edward
Talley, John
Tallsalt, Bert
Thomas, Edward
Thomas, Richard Sr.
Thompson, Clare M. Sr.
Thompson, Everett M.
Thompson, Francis T.
Thompson, Frank T.
Thompson, Nelson S.
Todacheene, Carl L.
Todacheenie, Frank
Tohe, Benson
Toledo, Bill Henry
Toledo, Curtis
Toledo, Frank
Toledo, Preston
Towne, Joseph H.
Towne, Zane
Tracy, Peter
Tso, Chester H.
Tso, Howard
Tso, Paul Edward
Tso, Samuel
Tsosie, Altred (KIA)
Tsosie, Cecil Gorman
Tsosie, Collins D.
Tsosie, David W.
Tsosie, Harry (KIA)
Tsosie, Howard (KIA)
Tsosie, Kenneth
Tsosie, Samuel Sr.
Tsosie, Woody B.
Upshaw, John
Upshaw, William R.
Vandever, Joe Sr.
Visalia, Buster

Wagner, Oliver
Walley, Robert
Werito, John
Whitman, Lyman J.
Willeto, Frank Jr.
Willetto, Frankie Chee
Willfe, John W. Jr.
Williams, Alex
Williams, Kenneth
Willie, George Boyd
Wilson, William Dean
Woodty, Clarence Bahi
Yazhe, Harrison A.
Yazza, Peter
Yazza, Vincent
Yazzie, Charley
Yazzie, Daniel
Yazzie, Eddie Melvin
Yazzie, Edison Kee
Yazzie, Francis
Yazzie, Frank Harold
Yazzie, Harding
Yazzie, Harrison A.
Yazzie, Joe Shorty
Yazzie, John
Yazzie, Justine D.
Yazzie, Lemuel Bahe
Yazzie, Ned
Yazzie, Pane D.
Yazzie, Peter
Yazzie, Raphael D.
Yazzie, Robert H.
Yazzie, Sam
Yazzie, William
Yazzle, Clifton
Yellowhair, Leon
Yellowhair, Stanley
Yellowman, Howard T.
Yoe, George
Zah, Henry

Names in bold – those surviving as of 2023
Names with highlighting - Killed in Action (KIA)

NAVAJO CODE TALKERS DICTIONARY

ALPHABET	NAVAJO WORD	LITERAL TRANSLATION
A	WOL-LA-CHEE	ANT
A	BE-LA-SANA	APPLE
A	TSE-NILL	AXE
B	NA-HASH-CHID	BADGER
B	SHUSH	BEAR
B	TOISH-JEH	BARREL
C	MOASI	CAT
C	TLA-GIN	COAL
C	BA-GOSHI	COW
D	BE	DEER
D	CHINDI	DEVIL
D	LHA-CHA-EH	DOG
E	AH-JAH	EAR
E	DZEH	ELK
E	AH-NAH	EYE
F	CHUO	FIR
F	TSA-E-DONIN-EE	FLY
F	MA-E	FOX
G	AH-TAD	GIRL
G	KLIZZIE	GOAT
G	JEHA	GUM
H	TSE-GAH	HAIR
H	CHA	HAT
H	LIN	HORSE
I	TKIN	ICE
I	YEH-HES	ITCH
I	A-CHI	INTESTINE
J	TKELE-CHO-G	JACKASS
J	AH-YA-TSINNE	JAW
J	YIL-DOI	JERK
K	JAD-HO-LONI	KETTLE
K	BA-AH-NE-DI-TININ	KEY
K	KLIZZIE-YAZZIE	KID
L	DIBEH-YAZZIE	LAMB
L	AH-JAD	LEG

ALPHABET	NAVAJO WORD	LITERAL TRANSLATION
L	NASH-DOIE-TSO	LION
M	TSIN-TLITI	MATCH
M	BE-TAS-TNI	MIRROR
M	NA-AS-TSO-SI	MOUSE
N	TSAH	NEEDLE
N	A-CHIN	NOSE
O	A-KHA	OIL
O	TLO-CHIN	ONION
O	NE-AHS-JAH	OWL
P	CLA-GI-AIH	PANT
P	BI-SO-DIH	PIG
P	NE-ZHONI	PRETTY
Q	CA-YEILTH	QUIVER
R	GAH	RABBIT
R	DAH-NES-TSA	RAM
R	AH-LOSZ	RICE
S	DIBEH	SHEEP
S	KLESH	SNAKE
T	D-AH	TEA
T	A-WOH	TOOTH
T	THAN-ZIE	TURKEY
U	SHI-DA	UNCLE
U	NO-DA-IH	UTE
V	A-KEH-DI-GLINI	VICTOR
W	GLOE-IH	WEASEL
X	AL-NA-AS-DZOH	CROSS
Y	TSAH-AS-ZIH	YUCCA
Z	BESH-DO-TLIZ	ZINC

NAMES OF VARIOUS ORGANISATIONS

ORGANISATIONS	NAVAJO WORD	LITERAL TRANSLATION
CORPS	DIN-NEH-IH	CLAN
DIVISION	ASHIH-HI	SALT
REGIMENT	TABAHA	EDGE WATER
BATTALION	TACHEENE	RED SOIL

ORGANISATIONS	NAVAJO WORD	LITERAL TRANSLATION
COMPANY	NAKIA	MEXICAN
PLATOON	HAS-CLISH-NIH	MUD
SECTION	YO-IH	BEADS
SQUAD	DEBEH-LI-ZINI	BLACK SHEEP

OFFICERS

RANK	NAVAJO WORD	LITERAL TRANSLATION
COMMANDING GEN.	BIH-KEH-HE (G)	WAR CHIEF
MAJOR GEN.	SO-NA-KIH	TWO STAR
BRIGADIER GEN.	SO-A-LA-IH	ONE STAR
COLONEL	ATSAH-BESH-LE-GAI	SILVER EAGLE
LT. COLONEL	CHE-CHIL-BE-TAH-BESH-LEGAI	SILVER OAK LEAF
MAJOR	CHE-CHIL-BE-TAH-OLA	GOLD OAK LEAF
CAPTAIN	BESH-LEGAI-NAH-KIH	TWO SILVER BARS
LIEUTENANT	BESH-LEGAI-A-LAH-IH	ONE SILVER BAR
COMMANDING OFFICER	HASH-KAY-GI-NA-TAH	WAR CHIEF
EXECUTIVE OFFICER	BIH-DA-HOL-NEHI	THOSE IN CHARGE

NAMES OF COUNTRIES

COUNTRY	NAVAJO WORD	LITERAL TRANSLATION
AFRICA	ZHIN-NI	BLACKIES
ALASKA	BEH-HGA	WITH WINTER
AMERICA	NE-HE-MAH	OUR MOTHER
AUSTRALIA	CHA-YES-DESI	ROLLED HAT
BRITAIN	TOH-TA	BETWEEN WATERS
CHINA	CEH-YEHS-BESI	BRAIDED HAIR
FRANCE	DA-GHA-HI	BEARD

COUNTRY	NAVAJO WORD	LITERAL TRANSLATION
GERMANY	BESH-BE-CHA-HE	IRON HAT
ICELAND	TKIN-KE-YAH	ICE LAND
INDIA	AH-LE-GAI	WHITE CLOTHES
ITALY	DOH-HA-CHI-YALI-TCHI	STUTTER
JAPAN	BEH-NA-ALI-TSOSIE	SLANT EYE
PHILIPPINE	KE-YAH-DA-NA-LHE	FLOATING ISLAND
RUSSIA	SILA-GOL-CHI-IH	RED ARMY
SOUTH AMERICA	SHA-DE-AH-NE-HI-MAH	SOUTH OUR MOTHER
SPAIN	DEBA-DE-NIH	SHEEP PAIN

NAMES OF AIRPLANES

AIRPLANE	NAVAJO WORD	LITERAL TRANSLATION
PLANES	WO-TAH-DE-NE-IH	AIR FORCE
DIVE BOMBER	GINI	CHICKEN HAWK
TORPEDO PLANE	TAS-CHIZZIE	SWALLOW
OBS. PLAN	NE-AS-JAH	OWL
FIGHTER PLANE	DA-HE-TIH-HI	HUMMING BIRD
BOMBER PLANE	JAY-SHO	BUZZARD
PATROL PLANE	GA-GIH	CROW
TRANSPORT	ATSAH	EAGLE

NAMES OF SHIPS

SHIP	NAVAJO WORD	LITERAL TRANSLATION
SHIPS	TOH-DINEH-IH	SEA FORCE
BATTLESHIP	LO-TSO	WHALE
AIRCRAFT	TSIDI-MOFFA-YE-HI	BIRD CARRIER
SUBMARINE	BESH-LO	IRON FISH
MINE SWEEPER	CHA	BEAVER
DESTROYER	CA-LO	SHARK

SHIP	NAVAJO WORD	LITERAL TRANSLATION
TRANSPORT	DINEH-NAY-YE-HI	MAN CARRIER
CRUISER	LO-TSO-YAZZIE	SMALL WHALE
MOSQUITO BOAT	TSE-E	MOSQUITO

NAMES OF MONTHS

MONTH	NAVAJO WORD	LITERAL TRANSLATION
JANUARY	ATSAH-BE-YAZ	SMALL EAGLE
FEBRUARY	WOZ-CHEIND	SQUEEKY VOICE
MARCH	TAH-CHILL	SMALL PLANT
APRIL	TAH-TSO	BIG PLANT
MAY	TAH-TSOSIE	SMALL PLANT
JUNE	BE-NE-EH-EH-JAH-TSO	BIG PLANTING
JULY	BE-NE-TA-TSOSIE	SMALL HARVEST
AUGUST	BE-NEEN-TA-TSO	BIG HARVEST
SEPTEMBER	GHAW-JIH	HALF
OCTOBER	NIL-CHI-TSOSIE	SMALL WIND
NOVEMBER	NIL-CHI-TSO	BIG WIND
DECEMBER	YAS-NIL-TES	CRUSTED SNOW

VOCABULARY

WORD	NAVAJO	LITERAL TRANSACTION
A		
ABANDON	YE-TSAN	RUN AWAY FROM
ABOUT	WOLA-CHI-A-MOFFA-GAHN	ANT FIGHT
ABREAST	WOLA-CHEE-BE-YIED	ANT BREAST
ACCOMPLISH	UL-SO	ALL DONE
ACCORDING	BE-KA-HO	ACCORDING TO
ACKNOWLEDGE	HANOT-DZIED	ACKNOWLEDGE
ACTION	AH-HA-TINH	PLACE OF ACTION
ACTIVITY	AH-HA-TINH-Y	ACTION ENDING IN Y

WORD	NAVAJO	LITERAL TRANSACTION
ADEQUATE	BEH-GHA	ENOUGH
ADDITION	IH-HE-DE-NDEL	ADDITION
ADDRESS	YI-CHIN-HA-TSE	ADDRESS
ADJACENT	BE-GAHI	NEAR
ADJUST	HAS-TAI-NEL-KAD	ADJUST
ADVANCE	NAS-SEY	AHEAD
ADVISE	NA-NETIN	ADVISE
AERIAL	BE-ZONZ	STINGER
AFFIRMATIVE	LANH	AFFIRMATIVE
AFTER	BI-KHA-DI (A)	AFTER
AGAINST	BE-NA-GNISH	AGAINST
AID	EDA-ELE-TSOOD	AID
AIR	NILCHI	AIR
AIRDOME	NILCHI-BEGHAN	AIRDOME
ALERT	HA-IH-DES-EE	ALERT
ALL	TA-A-TAH (A)	ALL
ALLIES	NIH-HI-CHO	ALLIES
ALONG	WOLACHEE-SNEZ	LONG ANT
ALSO	EH-DO	ALSO
ALTERNATE	NA-KEE-GO-NE-NAN-DEY-HE	SECOND POSITION
AMBUSH	KHAC-DA	AMBUSH
AMMUNITION	BEH-ELI-DOH-BE-CAH-ALI-TAS-AI	AMMUNITION
AMPHIBIOUS	CHAL	FROG
AND	DO	AND
ANGLE	DEE-CAHN	SLANTING
ANNEX	IH-NAY-TANI	ADDITION
ANNOUNCE	BEH-HA-O-DZE	ANNOUNCE
ANTI	WOL-LA-CHEE-TSIN	ANT ICE
ANTICIPATE	NI-JOL-LIH	ANTICIPATE
ANY	TAH-HA-DAH	ANY
APPEAR	YE-KA-HA-YA	APPEAR
APPROACH	BI-CHI-OL-DAH	APPROACH
APPROXIMATE	TO-KUS-DAN	APPROXIMATE
ARE	GAH-TSO BIG	RABBIT
AREA	HAZ-A-GIH	AREA

WORD	NAVAJO	LITERAL TRANSACTION
ARMOR	BESH-YE-HA-DA-DI-TEH	IRON PROTECTOR
ARMY	LEI-CHA-IH-YIL-KNEE-IH	ARMY
ARRIVE	IL-DAY	ARRIVE
ARTILLERY	BE-AL-DOH-TSO-LANI	MANY BIG GUNS
AS	AHCE	AS
ASSAULT	ALTSEH-E-JAH-HE	FIRST STRIKER
ASSEMBLE	DE-JI-KASH	BUNCH TOGETHER
ASSIGN	BAH-DEH-TAHN	ASSIGN
AT	AH-DI	AT
ATTACK	AL-TAH-JE-JAY	ATTACK
ATTEMPT	BO-O-NE-TAH (A)	TRY
ATTENTION	GIHA	ATTENTION
AUTHENTICATOR	HANI-BA-AH-HO-ZIN	KNOW ABOUT
AUTHORIZE	BE-BO-HO-SNEE	AUTHORIZE
AVAILABLE	TA-SHOZ-TEH-IH	AVAILABLE
B		
BAGGAGE	KLAILH (B)	BAGGAGE
BANZAI	NE-TAH	FOOL THEM
BARGE	BESH-NA-ELT	BARGE
BARRAGE	BESH-BA-WA-CHIND	BARRAGE
BARRIER	BIH-CHAN-NI-AH	IN THE WAY
BASE	BIH-TSEE-DIH	BASE
BATTERY	BIH-BE-AL-DOH-TKA-IH	THREE GUNS
BATTLE	DA-AH-HI-DZI-TSIO	BATTLE
BAY	TOH-AH-HI-GHINH	BAY
BAZOOKA	AH-ZHOL	BAZOOKA
BE	TSES-NAH	BEE
BEACH	TAH-BAHN (B)	BEACH
BEEN	TSES-NAH-NES-CHEE	BEE NUT
BEFORE	BIH-TSE-DIH	BEFORE
BEGIN	HA-HOL-ZIZ	COMMENCE FROM

WORD	NAVAJO	LITERAL TRANSACTION
BELONG	TSES-NAH-SNEZ	LONG BEE
BETWEEN	BI-TAH-KIZ	BETWEEN
BEYOND	BILH-LA DI	DOWN BELOW
BIVOUAC	EHL-NAS-TEH	BRUSH SHELTER
BOMB	A-YE-SHI	EGGS
BOOBY TRAP	DINEH-BA-WHOA-BLEHI	MAN TRAP
BORNE	YE-CHIE-TSAH	BORN ELK
BOUNDARY	KA-YAH-BI-NA-HAS-DZOH(B)	BOUNDARY
BULL DOZER	DOLA-ALTH-WHOSH	BULL SLEEP
BUNKER	TSAS-KA	SANDY HOLLOW
BUT	NEH-DIH	BUT
BY	BE-GHA	BY
C		
CABLE	BESH-LKOH	WIRE ROPE
CALIBER	NAHL-KIHD	MOVE AROUND
CAMP	TO-ALTSEH-HOGAN	TEMPORARY PLACE
CAMOUFLAGE	DI-NES-IH	HID
CAN	YAH-DI-ZINI	CAN
CANNONEER	BE-AL-DOH-TSO-DEY-DIL-DON-IGI	BIG GUN OPERATOR
CAPACITY	BE-NEL-AH	CAPACITY
CAPTURE	YIS-NAH	CAPTURE
CARRY	YO-LAILH	CARRY
CASE	BIT-SAH	CASE
CASUALTY	BIH-DIN-NE-DEY	PUT OUT OF ACTION
CAUSE	BI-NIH-NANI	CAUSE
CAVE	TSA-OND	ROCK CAVE
CEILING	DA-TEL-JAY	SEAL
CEMETARY	JISH-CHA	AMONG DEVILS
CENTER	ULH-NE-IH	CENTER
CHANGE	THLA-GO-A-NAT-ZAH	CHANGE
CHANNEL	HA-TALHI-YAZZIE	SMALL SINGER
CHARGE	AH-TAH-GI-JAH	CHARGE

WORD	NAVAJO	LITERAL TRANSACTION
CHEMICAL	TA-NEE	ALKALI
CIRCLE	NAS-PAS	CIRCLE
CIRCUIT	AH-HEH-HA-DAILH	CIRCUIT
CLASS	ALTH-AH-A-TEH	CLASS
CLEAR	YO-AH-HOL-ZHOD	CLEAR
CLIFF	TSE-YE-CHEE	CLIFF
CLOSE	UL-CHI-UH-NAL-YAH	CLOSE
COAST GUARD	TA-BAS-DSISSI	SHORE RUNNER
CODE	YIL-TAS	PECK
COLON	NAKI-ALH--DEH-DA-AL-ZHIN	TWO SPOTS
COLUMN	ALTH-KAY-NE-ZIH	COLUMN
COMBAT	DA-AH-HI-JIH-GANH	FIGHTING
COMBINATION	AL-TKAS-EI	MIXED
COME	HUC-QUO	COME
COMMA	TSA-NA-DAHL	TAIL DROP
COMMERCIAL	NAI-EL-NE-HI	COMMERCIAL
COMMIT	HUC-QUO-LA-JISH	COME GLOVE
COMMUNICATION	HA-NEH-AL-ENJI	MAKING TALK
CONCEAL	BE-KI-ASZ-JOLE	CONCEAL
CONCENTRATION	TA-LA-HI-JIH	ONE PLACE
CONCUSSION	WHE-HUS-DIL	CONCUSSION
CONDITION	AH-HO-TAI	HOW IT IS
CONFERENCE	BE-KE-YA-TI	TALK OVER
CONFIDENTIAL	NA-NIL-IN	KEPT SECRET
CONFIRM	TA-A-NEH	MAKE SURE
CONQUER	A-KEH-DES-DLIN	WON
CONSIDER	NE-TSA-CAS	THINK IT OVER
CONSIST	BILH (C)	CONSIST
CONSOLIDATE	AH-HIH-HI-NIL	PUT TOGETHER
CONSTRUCT	AHL-NEH	TO MAKE
CONTACT	AH-HI-DI-DAIL	COME TOGETHER
CONTINUE	TA-YI-TEH	CONTINUE
CONTROL	NAI-GHIZ	CONTROL
CONVOY	TKAL-KAH-O-NEL	MOVING ON WATER

WORD	NAVAJO	LITERAL TRANSACTION
COORDINATE	BEH-EH-HO-ZIN-NA-AS-DZOH	KNOWN LINES
COUNTER ATTACK	WOLTAH-AL-KI-GI-JEH	COUNTER ACT
COURSE	CO-JI-GOH	COURSE
CRAFT	AH-TOH	NEST
CREEK	TOH-NIL-TSANH	VERY LITTLE WATER
CROSS	AL-N-AS-DZOH	CROSS
CUB	SHUSH-YAHZ	CUB
D		
DASH	US-DZOH	DASH
DAWN	HA-YELI-KAHN	DAWN
DEFENSE	AH-KIN-CIL-TOH	DEFENSE
DEGREE	NAHL-KIHD	DEGREE
DELAY	BE-SITIHN	DEER LAY
DELIVER	BE-BIH-ZIHDE	DEER LIVER
DEMOLITION	AH-DEEL-TAHI	BLOW UP
DENSE	HO-DILH-CLA (D)	WET
DEPART	DA-DE-YAH	DEPART
DEPARTMENT	HOGAN	DEPARTMENT
DESIGNATE	YE-KHI-DEL-NEI	POINT OUT
DESPERATE	AH-DA-AH-HO-DZAH	DOWN TO LAST
DETACH	AL-CHA-NIL	DETACHED
DETAIL	BE-BEH-SHA	DEER TAIL
DETONATOR	AH-DEEL-TAHI (OR)	BLOWN UP
DIFFICULT	NA-NE-KLAH	DIFFICULT
DIG IN	LE-EH-GADE	DIG IN
DIRECT	AH-JI-GO	DIRECT
DISEMBARK	EH-HA-JAY	GET OUT
DISPATCH	LA-CHAI-EN-SEIS-BE-JAY	DOG IS PATCH
DISPLACE	HIH-DO-NAL	MOVE
DISPLAY	BE-SEIS-NA-NEH	DEER IS PLAY
DISPOSITION	A-HO-TEY	DISPOSITION
DISTRIBUTE	NAH-NEH	DISTRIBUTE
DISTRICT	BE-THIN-YA-NI-CHE	DEER ICE STRICT

99

WORD	NAVAJO	LITERAL TRANSACTION
DO	TSE-LE	SMALL PUP
DOCUMENT	BEH-EH-HO-ZINZ	DOCUMENT
DRIVE	AH-NOL-KAHL	DRIVE
DUD	DI-GISS-YAHZIE	SMALL DUMMY
DUMMY	DI-GISS-TSO	BIG DUMMY
E		
EACH	TA-LAHI-NE-ZINI-GO (D)	EACH
ECHELON	WHO-DZAH	LINE
EDGE	BE-BA-HI	EDGE
EFFECTIVE	BE-DELH-NEED	EFFECTIVE
EFFORT	YEA-GO	WITH ALL YOUR MIGHT
ELEMENT	AH-NA-NAI	TROOP REPRESENTING OTHERS
ELEVATE	ALI-KHI-HO-NE-OHA	ELEVATE
ELIMINATE	HA-BEH-TO-DZIL	ELIMINATE
EMBARK	EH-HO-JAY	GET ON
EMERGENCY	HO-NEZ-CLA	EMERGENCY
EMPLACEMENT	LA-AZ-NIL	EMPLACEMENT
ENCIRCLE	YE-NAS-TEH (E)	ENCIRCLE
ENCOUNTER	BI-KHANH	GO AGAINST
ENGAGE	A-HA-NE-HO-TA	AGREED
ENGINE	CHIDI-BI-TSI-TSINE (E)	ENGINE
ENGINEER	DAY-DIL-JAH-HE	ENGINEER
ENLARGE	NIH-TSA-GOH-AL-NEH	MAKE BIG
ENLIST	BIH-ZIH-A-DA-YI-LAH	ENLIST
ENTIRE	TA-A-TAH (E)	ENTIRE
ENTRENCH	E-GAD-AH-NE-LIH	MAKE DITCH
ENVELOP	A-ZAH-GI-YA	ENVELOP
EQUIPMENT	YA-HA-DE-TAHI	EQUIPMENT
ERECT	YEH-ZIHN	STAND UP
ESCAPE	A-ZEH-HA-GE-YAH	ESCAPE
ESTABLISH	HAS-TAY-DZAH	ESTABLISH

WORD	NAVAJO	LITERAL TRANSACTION
ESTIMATE	BIH-KE-TSE-HOD-DES-KEZ	ESTIMATE
EVACUATE	HA-NA	EVACUATE
EXCEPT	NEH-DIH (E)	EXCEPT
EXCEPT	NA-WOL-NE	EXPECT
EXCHANGE	ALH-NAHL-YAH	EXCHANGE
EXECUTE	A-DO-NIL	EXECUTE
EXPLOSIVE	AH-DEL-TAHI (E)	EXPLOSIVE
EXPEDITE	SHIL-LOH (E)	SPEED UP
EXTEND	NE-TDALE	MAKE WIDE
EXTREME	AL-TSAN-AH-BAHM	EACH END
F		
FAIL	CHA-AL-EIND	FAIL
FAILURE	YEES-GHIN	FAILURE
FARM	MAI-BE-HE-AHGAN	FOX ARM
FEED	DZEH-CHI-YON	FEED
FIELD	CLO-DIH (F)	FIELD
FIERCE	TOH-BAH-HA-ZSID	AFRAID
FILE	BA-EH-CHEZ	FILE
FINAL	TAH-AH-KWO-DIH	THAT IS ALL
FLAME THROWER	COH-AH-GHIL-TLID	FLAME THROWER
FLANK	DAH-DI-KAD	FLANK
FLARE	WO-CHI	LIGHT STREAK
FLIGHT	MA-E-AS-ZLOLI	FOX LIGHT
FORCE	TA-NA-NE-LADI	WITHOUT CARE
FORM	BE-CHA	FORM
FORMATION	BE-CHA-YE-LAILH	FORMATION
FORTIFICATION	AH-NA-SOZI	CLIFF DWELLING
FORTIFY	AH-NA-SOZI-YAZZIE	SMALL FORTIFICATION
FORWARD	TEHI	LET'S GO
FRAGMENTATION	BESH-YAZZIE	SMALL METAL
FREQUENCY	HA-TALHI-TSO	BIG SINGER
FRIENDLY	NEH-HECHO-DA-NE	FRIENDLY
FROM	BI-TSAN-DEHN	FROM
FURNISH	YEAS-NIL (F)	FURNISH
FURTHER	WO-NAS-DI	FURTHER

WORD	NAVAJO	LITERAL TRANSACTION
G		
GARRISON	YAH-A-DA-HAL-YON-IH	TAKE CARE OF
GASOLINE	CHIDI-BI-TOH	GASOLINE
GRENADE	NI-MA-SI	POTATOES
GUARD	NI-DIH-DA-HI	GUARD
GUIDE	NAH-E-THLAI	GUIDE
H		
HALL	LHI-TA-A-TA	HORSE ALL
HALF TRACK	ALH-NIH-JAH-A-QUHE	RACE TRACK
HALT	TA-AKWAI-I	HALT
HANDLE	BET-SEEN	HANDLE
HAVE	JO	HAVE
HEADQUARTER	NA-HA-TAH-TA-BA-HOGAN	HEADQUARTER
HELD	WO-TAH-TA-EH-DAHN-OH	HELD (PAST TENSE)
HIGH	WO-TAH	HIGH
HIGH EXPLOSIVE	BE-AL-DOH-BE-CA-BIH-DZIL-IGI	POWERFUL SHELL
HIGHWAY	WO-TAH-HO-NE-TEH	HIGH WAY
HOLD	WO-TKANH	HOLD
HOSPITAL	A-ZEY-AL-IH	PLACE OF MEDICINE
HOSTILE	A-NAH-NE-DZIN	NOT FRIENDLY
HOWITZER	BE-EL-DON-TS-QUODI	SHORT BIG GUN
I		
ILLUMINATE	WO-CHI (I)	LIGHT UP
IMMEDIATELY	SHIL-LOH (I)	IMMEDIATELY
IMPACT	A-HE-DIS-GOH	IMPACT
IMPORTANT	BA-HAS-TEH	IMPORTANT
IMPROVE	HO-DOL-ZHOND	IMPROVE
INCLUDE	EL-TSOD	INCLUDE

WORD	NAVAJO	LITERAL TRANSACTION
INCREASE	HO-NALH	INCREASE
INDICATE	BA-HAL-NEH	TELL ABOUT
INFANTRY	TA-NEH-NAL-DAHI	INFANTRY
INFILTRATE	YE-GHA-NE-JEH	WENT THROUGH
INITIAL	BEH-ED-DE-DLID	BRAND
INSTALL	EHD-TNAH	INSTALL
INSTALLATION	NAS-NIL	IN PLACE
INSTRUCT	NA-NE-TGIN	TEACH
INTELLIGENCE	HO-YA (I)	SMART
INTENSE	DZEEL	STRENGTH
INTERCEPT	YEL-NA-ME-JAH	INTERCEPT
INTERFERE	AH-NILH-KHLAI	INTERFERE
INTERPRET	AH-TAH-HA-NE	INTERPRET
INVESTIGATE	NA-ALI-KA	TRACK
INVOLVE	A-TAH	INVOLVOE
IS	SEIS	SEVEN
ISLAND	SEIS-KEYAH	SEVEN ISLAND
ISOLATE	BIH-TSA-NEL-KAD	SEPARATE
J		
JUNGLE	WOH-DI-CHIL	JUNGLE
K		
KILL	NAZ-TSAID	KILL
KILOCYCLE	NAS-TSAID-A-KHA-AH-YEH-HA-DILH	KILL OIL GO AROUND
L		
LABOR	NA-NISH (L)	LABOR
LAND	KAY-YAH	LAND
LAUNCH	TKA-GHIL-ZHOD	LAUNCH
LEADER	AH-NA-GHAI	LEADER
LEAST	DE-BE-YAZIE-HA-A-AH	LAMB FEAST
LEAVE	DAH-DE-YAH	HE LEFT
LEFT	NISH-CLA-JIH-GOH	LEFT
LESS	BI-OH (L)	LESS
LEVEL	DIL-KONH	LEVEL

WORD	NAVAJO	LITERAL TRANSACTION
LIAISON	DA-A-HE-GI-ENEH	KNOW OTHER'S ACTION
LIMIT	BA-HAS-AH	LIMIT
LITTER	NI-DAS-TON (L)	SCATTER
LOCATE	A-KWE-EH	SPOT
LOSS	UT-DIN	LOSS
M		
MACHINE GUN	A-KNAH-AS-DONIH	RAPID FIRE GUN
MAGNETIC	NA-E-LAHI	PICK UP
MANAGE	HASTNI-BEH-NA-HAI	MAN AGE
MANEUVER	NA-NA-O-NALTH	MOVING AROUND
MAP	KAH-YA-NESH-CHAI	MAP
MAXIMUM	BEL-DIL-KHON	FILL TO TOP
MECHANIC	CHITI-A-NAYL-INIH	AUTO REPAIRMAN
MECHANIZED	CHIDI-DA-AH-HE-GONI	FIGHTING CARS
MEDICAL	A-ZAY	MEDICINE
MEGACYCLE	MIL-AH-HEH-AH-DILH	MILLION GO AROUND
MERCHANT SHIP	NA-EL-NEHI-TSIN-NA-AILH	MERCHANT SHIP
MESSAGE	HANE-AL-NEH	MESSAGE
MILITARY	SILAGO-KEH-GOH	MILITARY
MILLIMETER	NA-AS-TSO-SI-A-YE-DO-TISH	DOUBLE MOUSE
MINE	HA-GADE	MINE
MINIMUM	BE-OH (M)	MINIMUM
MINUTE	AH-KHAY-EL-KIT-YAZZIE	LITTLE HOUR
MISSION	AL-NESHODI	MISSION
MISTAKE	O-ZHI	MISS
MOPPING	HA-TAO-DI	MOPPING
MORE	THLA-NA-NAH	MORE
MORTAR	BE-AL-DOH-CID-DA-HI	SITTING GUN
MOTION	NA-HOT-NAH	MOTION

WORD	NAVAJO	LITERAL TRANSACTION
MOTOR	CHIDE-BE-TSE-TSEN	CAR HEAD
N		
NATIVE	KA-HA-TENI	NATIVE
NAVY	TAL-KAH-SILAGO	SEA SOLDIER
NECESSARY	YE-NA-ZEHN	WANT
NEGATIVE	DO-YA-SHO-DA	NO GOOD
NET	NA-NES-DIZI	NET
NEUTRAL	DO-NEH-LINI	NEUTRAL
NORMAL	DOH-A-TA-H-DAH	NORMAL
NOT	NI-DAH-THAN-ZIE	NO TURKEY
NOTICE	NE-DA-TAZI-THIN	NO TURKEY ICE
NOW	KUT	NOW
NUMBER	BEH-BIH-KE-AS-CHINIGH	WHAT'S WRITTEN
O		
OBJECTIVE	BI-NE-YEI	GOAL
OBSERVE	HAL-ZID	OBSERVE
OBSTACLE	DA-HO-DESH-ZHA	OBSTACLE
OCCUPY	YEEL-TSOD	TAKEN
OF	TOH-NI-TKAL-LO	OCEAN FISH
OFFENSIVE	BIN-KIE-JINH-JIH-DEZ-JAY	OFFENSIVE
ONCE	TA-LAI-DI	ONCE
ONLY	TA-EI-TAY-A-YAH	ONLY
OPERATE	YE-NAHL-NISH	WORK AT
OPPORTUNITY	ASH-GA-ALIN	OPPORTUNITY
OPPOSITION	NE-HE-TSAH-JIH-SHIN	OPPOSITION
OR	EH-DO-DAH-GOH	EITHER
ORANGE	TCHIL-LHE-SOI	ORANGE
ORDER	BE-EH-HO-ZINI	ORDER
ORDNANCE	LEI-AZ-JAH	UNDER GROUND
ORIGINATE	DAS-TEH-DO	BEGIN
OTHER	LA-E-CIH	OTHER
OUT	CLO-DIH	OUT SIDE

WORD	NAVAJO	LITERAL TRANSACTION
OVERLAY	BE-KA-HAS-TSOZ	OVERLAY
P		
PARENTHESIS	ATSANH	RIB
PARTICULAR	A-YO-AD-DO-NEH	PARTICULAR
PARTY	DA-SHA-JAH	PARTY
PAY	NA-ELI-YA	PAY
PENALIZE	TAH-NI-DES-TANH	SET BACK
PERCENT	YAL	MONEY
PERIOD	DA-AHL-ZHIN	PERIOD
PERIODIC	DA-AL-ZHIN-THIN-MOASI	PERIOD ICE CAT
PERMIT	GOS-SHI-E	PERMIT
PERSONNEL	DA-NE-LEI	MEMBER
PHOTOGRAPH	BEH-CHI-MA-HAD-NIL	PHOTOGRAPH
PILL BOX	BI-SO-DIH-DOT-SAHI-BI-TSAH	SICK PIG BOX
PINNED DOWN	BIL-DAH-HAS-TANH-YA	PINNED DOWN
PLANE	TSIDI	BIRD
PLASMA	DIL-DI-GHILI	PLASMA
POINT	BE-SO-DE-DEZ-AHE	PIG POINT
PONTOON	TKOSH-JAH-DA-NA-ELT	FLOATING BARREL
POSITION	BILH-HAS-AHN	POSITION
POSSIBLE	TA-HA-AH-TAY	POSSIBLE
POST	SAH-DEI	POST
PREPARE	HASH-TAY-HO-DIT-NE	PREPARE
PRESENT	KUT	PRESENT
PREVIOUS	BIH-TSE-DIH	PREVIOUS
PRIMARY	ALTSEH-NAN-DAY-HI-GIH	1ST POSTION
PRIORITY	HANE-PESODI	PRIORITY
PROBABLE	DA-TSI	PROBABLE
PROBLEM	NA-NISH-TSOH	BIG JOB
PROCEED	NAY-NIH-JIH	GO

WORD	NAVAJO	LITERAL TRANSACTION
PROGRESS	NAH-SAI	PROGRESS
PROTECT	AH-CHANH	SELF DEFENSE
PROVIDE	YIS-NIL	PROVIDE
PURPLE	DINL-CHI	PURPLE
PYROTECHNIC	COH-NA-CHANH	FANCY FIRE
Q		
QUESTION	AH-JAH	EAR
QUICK	SHIL-LOH	QUICK
R		
RADAR	ESAT-TSANH (R)	LISTEN
RAID	DEZJAY	RAID
RAILHEAD	A-DE-GEH-HI	SHIPPING POINT
RAILROAD	KONH-NA-AL-BANSI-BI-THIN	RAILROAD
RALLYING	A-LAH-NA-O-GLALIH	GATHERING
RANGE	AN-ZAH	DISTANCE
RATE	GAH-EH-YAHN	RABBIT ATE
RATION	NA-A-JAH	RATION
RAVINE	CHUSH-KA (R)	RAVINE
REACH	IL-DAY (R)	REACH
READY	KUT (R)	READY
REAR	BE-KA-DENH (R)	REAR
RECEIPT	SHOZ-TEH	RECEIPT
RECOMMEND	CHE-HO-TAI-TAHN	RECOMMEND
RECONNAISSANCE	HA-A-CIDI	INSPECTOR
RECONNOITER	TA-HA-NE-AL-YA	MAKE SURE
RECORD	GAH-AH-NAH-KLOLI	R-E-ROPE
RED	LI-CHI	RED
REEF	TSA-ZHIN	BLACK ROCK
REEMBARK	EH-NA-COH	GO IN
REFIRE	NA-NA-COH	REFIRE
REGULATE	NA-YEL-N	REGULATE
REINFORCE	NAL-DZIL	REINFORCE
RELIEF	AGANH-TOL-JAY	RELIEF
RELIEVE	NAH-JIH-CO-NAL-YA	REMOVE
REORGANIZE	HA-DIT-ZAH	REORGANIZE

WORD	NAVAJO	LITERAL TRANSACTION
REPLACEMENT	NI-NA-DO-NIL	REPLACEMENT
REPORT	WHO-NEH	GOT WORD
REPRESENTATIVE	TKA-NAZ-NILI	TRIPLE MEN
REQUEST	JO-KAYED-GOH	ASK FOR
RESERVE	HESH-J-E	RESERVE
RESTRICT	BA-HO-CHINI	RESTRICT
RETIRE	AH-HOS-TEEND	RETIRE
RETREAT	JI-DIN-NES-CHANH	RETREAT
RETURN	NA-DZAH	CAME BACK
REVEAL	WHO-NEH (L)	REVEAL
REVERT	NA-SI-YIZ	TURN ABOUT
REVETMENT	BA-NAS-CLA (R)	CORNER
RIDGE	GAH-GHIL-KEID	RABBIT RIDGE
RIFLEMAN	BE-AL-DO-HOSTEEN	RIFLEMEN
RIVER	TOH-YIL-KAL	MUCH WATER
ROBOT BOMB	A-YE-SHI-NA-TAH-IH	EGG FLY
ROCKET	LESZ-YIL-BESHI	SAND BOIL
ROLL	YEH-MAS	ROLL
ROUND	NAZ-PAS (R)	ROUND
ROUTE	GAH-BIH-TKEEN	RABBIT TRAIL
RUNNER	NIH-DZID-TEIH	RUNNER
S		
SABOTAGE	A-TKEL-YAH	HINDERED
SABOTEUR	A-TKEL-EL-INI	TROUBLE MAKER
SAILOR	CHA-LE-GAI	WHITE CAPS
SALVAGE	NA-HAS-GLAH	PICK THEM UP
SAT	BIH-LA-SANA-CID-DA-HI	APPLE SITTING
SCARLET	REDLHE-CHI (S & R)	RED
SCHEDULE	BEH-EH-HO-ZINI	SCHEDULE
SCOUT	HA-A-SID-AL-SIZI-GIH	SHORT RACOON
SCREEN	BESH-NA-NES-DIZI	SCREEN
SEAMAN	TKAL-KAH-DINEH-IH	SEAMAN
SECRET	BAH-HAS-TKIH	SECRET

WORD	NAVAJO	LITERAL TRANSACTION
SECTOR	YOEHI (S)	SECTOR
SECURE	YE-DZHE-AL-TSISI	SMALL SECURITY
SEIZE	YEEL-STOD	SEIZE
SELECT	BE-TAH-HAS-GLA	TOOK OUT
SEMI COLON	DA-AHL-ZHIN-BI-TSA-NA-DAHL	DOT DROP
SET	DZEH-CID-DA-HI	ELK SITTING
SHACKLE	DI-BAH-NESH-GOHZ	SHACKLE
SHELL	BE-AL-DOH-BE-CA	SHELL
SHORE	TAH-BAHN (S)	SHORE
SHORT	BOSH-KEESH	SHORT
SIDE	BOSH-KEESH	SIDE
SIGHT	YE-EL-TSANH	SEEN
SIGNAL	NA-EH-EH-GISH	BY SIGNS
SIMPLEX	ALAH-IH-NE-TIH	INNER WIRE
SIT	TKIN-CID-DA-HI	ICE SITTING
SITUATE	A-HO-TAY	(S) SITUATE
SMOKE	LIT	SMOKE
SNIPER	OH-BEHI	PICK 'EM OFF
SPACE	BE-TKAH	BETWEEN
SPECIAL	E-YIH-SIH	MAIN THING
SPEED	YO-ZONS	SWIFT MOTION
SPORADIC	AH-NA-HO-NEIL	NOW AND THEN
SPOTTER	EEL-TSAY-I	SPOTTER
SPRAY	KLESH-SO-DILZIN	SNAKE PRAY
SQUADRON	NAH-GHIZI	SQUASH
STORM	NE-OL	STORM
STRAFF	NA-WO-GHI-GOID	HOE
STRAGGLER	CHY-NE-DE-DAHE	STRAGGLER
STRATEGY	NA-HA-TAH (S)	STRATEGY
STREAM	TOH-NI-LIH	RUNNING WATER
STRENGTH	DZHEL	STRENGTH
STRETCH	DESZ-TSOOD	STRETCH
STRIKE	NAY-DAL-GHAL	STRIKE
STRIP	HA-TIH-JAH	STRIP
STUBBORN	NIL-TA	STUBBORN
SUBJECT	NA-NISH-YAZZIE	SMALL JOB

WORD	NAVAJO	LITERAL TRANSACTION
SUBMERGE	TKAL-CLA-YI-YAH	WENT UNDER WATER
SUBMIT	A-NIH-LEH	SEND
SUBORDINATE	AL-KHI-NAL-DZL	HELPING EACH OTHER
SUCCEED	YAH-TAY-GO-E-ELAH	MAKE GOOD
SUCCESS	UT-ZAH	IT IS DONE
SUCCESSFUL	UT-ZAH-HA-DEZ-BIN	IT IS DONE WELL
SUCCESSIVE	UT-ZAH-SID	SUCCESS SCAR
SUCH	YIS-CLEH	SOX
SUFFER	TO-HO-NE	SUFFER
SUMMARY	SHIN-GO-BAH	SUMMER MARY
SUPPLEMENTARY	TKA-GO-NE-NAN-DEY-HE	3RD POSITION
SUPPLY	NAL-YEH-HI	SUPPLY
SUPPLY SHIP	NALGA-HI-TSIN-NAH-AILH	SUPPLY SHIP
SUPPORT	BA-AH-HOT-GLI	DEPEND
SURRENDER	NE-NA-CHA	SURRENDER
SURROUND	NAZ-PAS (S)	SURROUND
SURVIVE	YIS-DA-YA	SURVIVE
SYSTEM	DI-BA-TSA-AS-ZHI-BI-TSIN	SYSTEM
T		
TACTICAL	E-CHIHN	TACTICAL
TAKE	GAH-TAHN	TAKE
TANK	CHAY-DA-GAHI	TORTOISE
TANK DESTROYER	CHAY-DA-GAHI-NAIL-TSAIDI	TORTOISE KILLER
TARGET	WOL-DONI	TARGET
TASK	TAZI-NA-EH-DIL-KID	TURKEY ASK
TEAM	DEH-NA-AS-TSO-SI	TEA MOUSE
TERRACE	ALI-KHI-HO-NE-OHA (T)	TERRACE
TERRAIN	TASHI-NA-HAL-THIN	TURKEY RAIN
TERRITORY	KA-YAH (T)	TERRITORY
THAT	TAZI-CHA	TURKEY HAT
THE	CHA-GEE	BLUE-JAY

WORD	NAVAJO	LITERAL TRANSACTION
THEIR	BIH	THEIR
THEREAFTER	TA-ZI-KWA-I-BE-KA-DI	TURKEY HERE AFTER
THESE	CHA-GI-O-EH	THE SEE
THEY	CHA-GEE (Y)	THE Y
THIS	DI	THE
TOGETHER	TA-BILH	TOGETHER
TORPEDO	LO-BE-CA	FISH SHELL
TOTAL	TA-AL-SO	TOTAL
TRACER	BEH-NA-AL-KAH-HI	TRACER
TRAFFIC DIAGRAM	HANE-BA-NA-AS-DZOH	DIAGRAM STORY LINE
TRAIN	COH-NAI-ALI-BAHN-SI	TRAIN
TRANSPORTATION	A-HAH-DA-A-CHA	TRANSPORTATION
TRENCH	E-GADE	TRENCH
TRIPLE	TKA-IH	TRIPLE
TROOP	NAL-DEH-HI	TROOP
TRUCK	CHIDO-TSO	BIG AUTO
TYPE	ALTH-AH-A-TEH	TYPE
U		
UNDER	BI-YAH	UNDER
UNIDENTIFIED	DO-BAY-HOSEN-E	UNIDENTIFIED
UNIT	DA-AZ-JAH (U)	UNIT
UNSHACKLE	NO-DA-EH-NESH-GOHZ	UNSHACKLE
UNTIL	UH-QUO-HO	UNTIL
V		
VICINITY	NA-HOS-AH-GIH	THERE ABOUT
VILLAGE	CHAH-HO-OH-LHAN-IH	MANY SHELTER
VISIBILITY	NAY-ES-TEE	VISIBILITY
VITAL	TA-EH-YE-SY	VITAL
W		
WARNING	BILH-HE-NEH (W)	WARNING

WORD	NAVAJO	LITERAL TRANSACTION
WAS	NE-TEH	WAS
WATER	TKOH	WATER
WAVE	YILH-KOLH	WAVE
WEAPON	BEH-DAH-A-HI-JIH-GANI	FIGHTING WEAPON
WELL	TO-HA-HA-DLAY	WELL
WHEN	GLOE-EH-NA-AH-WO-HAI	WEASEL HEN
WHERE	GLOE-IH-QUI-AH	WEASEL HERE
WHICH	GLOE-IH-A-HSI-TLON	WEASEL TIED TOGETHER
WILL	GLOE-IH-DOT-SAHI	SICK WEASEL
WIRE	BESH-TSOSIE	SMALL WIRE
WITH	BILH (W)	WITH
WITHIN	BILH-BIGIH	WITH IN
WITHOUT	TA-GAID	WITHOUT
WOOD	CHIZ	FIRE WOOD
WOUND	CAH-DA-KHI	WOUND
Y		
YARD	A-DEL-TAHL	YARD
Z		
ZONE	BIH-NA-HAS-DZOH	ZONE

BIBLIOGRAPHY

BOOKS USED FOR REFERENCE

- "Code Talker" by Chester Nez with Judith Schiess Avila
- "Navajo Weapon" by Sally McClain
- "Code Talker": The First and Only Memoir by One of the Original Navajo Code Talkers of WWII

WEBSITES USED AS REFERENCE

- http://genealogytrails.com/ww2/codetalkers_index.html
- http://www.nativepartnership.org/site/PageServer?pagename=swirc_hist_dustbowl
- https://en.wikipedia.org/wiki/American_Indian_boarding_schools
- https://en.wikipedia.org/wiki/Aryan_race
- https://en.wikipedia.org/wiki/File:Navajo_Code_Talker_Memorial.jpg
- https://en.wikipedia.org/wiki/Fort_Defiance,_Arizona
- https://en.wikipedia.org/wiki/Ira_Hayes
- https://en.wikipedia.org/wiki/List_of_Native_American_boarding_schools
- https://en.wikipedia.org/wiki/Long_Walk_of_the_Navajo
- https://en.wikipedia.org/wiki/Native_American_jewelry
- https://en.wikipedia.org/wiki/Navajo
- https://en.wikipedia.org/wiki/Navajo_medicine
- https://en.wikipedia.org/wiki/Navajo_Nation
- https://en.wikipedia.org/wiki/Navajo-Churro
- https://en.wikipedia.org/wiki/Oljato%E2%80%93Monument_Valley,_Utah
- https://en.wikipedia.org/wiki/Scorched_earth
- https://en.wikipedia.org/wiki/Shackle_code
- https://en.wikipedia.org/wiki/Tripartite_Pact
- https://en.wiktionary.org/wiki/Appendix:Navajo_code_talkers%27_dictionary
- https://georgewbush-whitehouse.archives.gov/index.html
- https://simple.wikipedia.org/wiki/Embargo
- https://www.alivehospice.org/news-events/culture-and-death-native-american-heritage

- https://www.archives.gov/publications/prologue/2001/winter/navajo-code-talkers.html
- https://www.history.navy.mil/research/library/online-reading-room/title-list-alphabetically/n/navajo-code-talker-dictionary.html
- https://www.journals.uchicago.edu/doi/pdf/10.1086/275311
- https://www.morrissett.com/no-word-for-goodbye
- https://ww2.gvsu.edu/walll/Japan NO SURRENDER.htm
- https:genealogytrails.com/ww2/codetalkers_listofnames.html

IMAGES USED

Part of cover image	
Part of cover image	
Navajo dress Part of cover image, 2	
Part of cover image	
Part of cover image See Foreword	
Holiday photo 2023 See Foreword	
Friendship See Foreword, 13	
Clans Page 1	

Coloured corn Page 3	
Navajo woman with corn Page 3	
Frybread Page 4	
Navajo woman weaving Page 4, 35	
Navajo Hogan Page 5	
Map of Navajo sacred lands Page 6	
Holy People diagram Page 7	
Image similar to corn pollen Page 8	

Silver jewellery maker Page 11	
Navajo bracelets Page 11	
My Navajo jewellery Page 11	
Good luck Swastika Page 12	
Spiral Hand - Health and good fortune Page 13	
Map of Navajo lands Page 14	
My Book Trail of Tears Page 15	
Map of The Long Walk Page 16	

Colonel 'Kit' Carson Page 18	
Map of the Long Walk Page 18, 20	
Navajo people on The Long Walk Page 19	
Navajo leaders on The Long Walk Page 20	
Soldiers guarding Navajo Page 21	
Navajo captives at Fort Sumner Page 21	
Treaty marker Page 23	
Manuelito Page 24	

Treaty document Page 24	
Navajo Reservation Page 26	
Long Walk mural Page 26	
School Page 27	
Fort Defiance Page 30	
Navajo medicine man Nesjaja Hatali, 1907 Page 31	
School Page 32	
Churro sheep Page 33	

Churro sheep Page 33		
Navajo Code Talkers Page 47		
Navajo Code Talker Page 48		
Map of the Western Pacific area, 1942 Page 51		
Marines at Guadalcanal Page 51		
Henderson Field Page 52		
First on the beaches Page 52		
Pacific Islands crab Page 53		

Fatalities on the beach Page 54		
Crocodile Page 55		
Drawing of Marine in dugout Page 55		
Code Talkers at work Page 56		
Map of Bougainville Page 60		
USMC Code Talkers Page 61		
3rd Marine Division, 2nd Raider's sign on Bougainville Page 61		
Cooking Page 62		

Seventh War Loan Drive Poster (May 11th –July 4th, 1945) Page 67	
Pfc Ira Hayes Page 67	
Raising the Flag Page 68	
Navajo Code Talkers uniform Page 69	
Bill Toledo, Robert Walley and Alfred Newman Page 71	
Navajo Code Talker Memorial Page 72, 79	
Navajo Nation WW II Memorial Page 73	
Chester Nez Page 75	

Purple Heart Page 74	
Peter MacDonald Page 75	
Thomas H. Begay Page 75	
Code Talkers Monument Page 76	
Totem Pole Monument Valley Page 78	
Feather Image by Clker-Free-Vector-Images from Pixabay Used Throughout	

INDEX

ALSO AVAILABLE BY CAROL DEAN

The Comanche were the fiercest and most feared of tribes. A warring tribe.

And a tribe, a people, fighting to preserve their traditions, values and the land they loved.

Find out how such a tribe lived their everyday lives, and how the Comanche almost fell into obscurity with the help of the 'white man', and how they rose again to be the Comanche Nation that they are today.

Available in hardback or paperback – black and white or colour.

Sitting Bull was born in 1831 in a time when the white man had descended on the Sioux tribal lands and claimed it for themselves. A turbulent time that continued throughout his life. A life of devotion to his family, caring for his tribe, courageous and brave in the face of danger and a gifted communicator with the animals and the Great Spirit.

His tribe held him in high esteem and spoke of his 'big medicine' which was a huge compliment to the man.

And that's only a small part of the man himself. Learn about the legend that was and is Chief Sitting Bull and perhaps you too will admire the man he became.

Available in hardback or paperback – black and white or colour.

Over the years the Apache have been led by many legendary people. Two well known Apache legends, and the two that I have chosen to write about, are Geronimo and Cochise.

They lived in turbulent times. Times when these two legends needed to join forces to fight for their lands and the lives of their people against the Mexican and the American soldiers. Both forces seeking revenge and retribution for the deaths of loved ones at the hands of the white man's army, and the loss of their sacred lands desecrated by the white man.

Geronimo and Cochise's joint forces became a daring, dynamic and powerful fighting force to be reckoned with and feared.

This is their story.

Available in hardback or paperback – black and white or colour

Carol Dean's book takes you back to the days of the Comanche and their struggle against the white man. Quanah Parker became one man living in two worlds as he was the last chief the Comanche ever had.

This book takes the reader through Parker's assimilation into the white man's world and the great success he made of it and describes how he became a major part of American history and still is today.

Carol's book "Comanche Life" contains a brief summary of Quanah's life as he was the last chief of the Comanche. This book provides a fuller picture of this incredible man.

In the year 1830 President Andrew Jackson signed and had approved the Indian Removal Act. For the Five Civilised Tribes of Native America, the Choctaw, Chickasaw, Seminole, Muscagee (Creek), and the Cherokee, this meant the end of their lives as they knew it and the start of the Trail of Tears.

A trail that, not only brought tears, but has become famous for the starvation, disease, despair and death amongst the Five Civilised Tribes that were forced to travel on it.

An unbelievably sad story, said to be the most sorrowful legacy of the Jacksonian Era.

But it's all true.

The Native American has for many hundreds of years fought long and hard through many battles and suffered broken treaties to try to hold onto their lands and traditions. Many famous Native Americans have been noted and credited for the successes, or failures, of some of those well known battles. Names that we all know and recognise, and will live on in history forever.

But there are others, perhaps not so famous, who played their part in the Native American history. This book mentions just some of them. A few that I personally have chosen to honour, through this book, for their part. And there are many, many more.

Read how history was shaped as *They Too Played Their Part*.

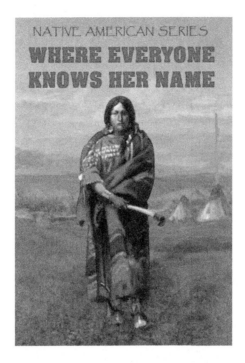

Many famous battles throughout Native American and American history have been fought with both sides gaining victories or incurring losses. But those battles were fought by many famous warriors of the time. And not all of them were male warriors.

This book entitled, 'Where Everyone Knows Her Name' delves into the lives and the bravery of some of the female warriors fighting alongside their male compatriots and winning through in those battles.

Some names you will recognise, and some will be new to you. But put them altogether and read about the courage, determination, and valour these female warriors showed in the face of danger. This book covers only a few of these impressive and powerful women in history. Women that I have personally chosen to write about. It's to remember those women and all the others in history too. And there are so many more.

When reading about Native Americans, not many will consider exactly what Native Americans are doing now. That's understandable considering the appalling history of battles for lands, traditions, and their cultures under the white man's hands. No set of peoples or civilisations have ever had to face such trauma as the Native Americans have for hundreds of years. That's the history that is read about, understood, and hopefully learnt from so that it never happens again.

But Native Americans have come through everything that they have had thrown at them over the years, and are now making a new history. A history of renewed interest and learning in their cultures, language, traditions, and their turbulent past. With many Native Americans reaching great heights in a very competitive world.

This book covers that new Native American history and honours just some of those involved.

Carol's book charts the lives and times of the American expansion into the west during the 19th century. A hard life for many but it paved the way for a new life and new opportunities to find the American Dream.

Some of the names you may recognise as they are now legends among frontier men, gunslingers and card sharps. These legends not only made the West wild, but have been immortalised in films and books, making the Wild West so fascinating even now.

Printed in Great Britain
by Amazon

38446484R00086